lonely planet

Rocky Mountains & Pacific Northwest's

NATIONAL PARKS

T0054605

Contents

COVID-19

We have re-checked every business in this book before publication to ensure that it is still open after the COVID-19 outbreak. However, the economic and social impacts of COVID-19 will continue to be felt long after the outbreak has been contained, and many businesses, services and events referenced in this guide may experience ongoing restrictions. Some businesses may be temporarily closed, have changed their opening hours and services, or require bookings; some unfortunately could have closed permanently. We suggest you check with venues before visiting for the latest information.

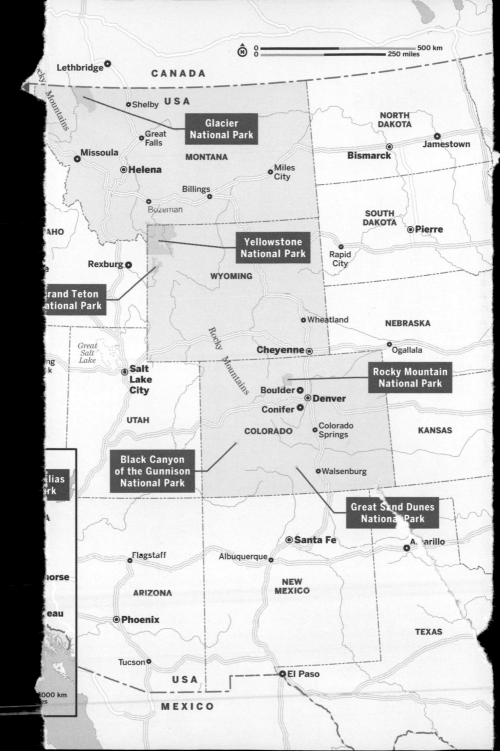

Welcome to Rocky Mountains & Pacific Northwest's National Parks

The national parks of the Rockies, the Pacific Northwest and Alaska are the very essence of America, superb natural expanses that reflect so many facets of this vast, complex and magnificently diverse country.

National parks are America's big backyards. No cross-country road trip would be complete without a visit to at least one of these remarkable natural treasures, rich in unspoiled wilderness, rare wildlife and drama-filled history.

The parks represent American ideals at their best. That we are able to enjoy these special places today may seem like a matter of course, but the establishment of the national park system was no sure thing. Challenges have been present every step of the way, and many threatened to derail the entire experiment. But, until now, the best instincts of a nation have prevailed. And it's not just the parks: there's also an incredible portfolio of federally protected areas numbering in their thousands.

The Rockies and the Pacific Northwest are especially blessed when it comes to some of America's most storied (and most beautiful, most wildlife-rich) parks. In fact, their names read like a greatest hits of the US: Yellowstone, Grand Teton, Rocky Mountain, Glacier, Olympic, Mt Rainier... Then there are some lesser-known jewels that deserve to be stars in their own right, from Crater Lake or North Cascades to Black Canyon of the Gunnison and Great Sand Dunes. And over 1500 miles to the north lies wilder, remoter Alaska whose eight national parks cover 54 million acres.

Whether you're looking for wolves and grizzlies in Yellowstone, exploring some of the world's most shapely mountains in Grand Teton or taking in the views along Glacier National Park's Going-to-the-Sun Road, getting to know this region is akin to a concentrated grand tour of some of the country's grandest natural spectacles.

No cross-country road trip would be complete without a visit to one of these treasures

Glacier National Park (p140)
BKAMPRATH/GETTY IMAGES/ISTOCKPHOTO ©

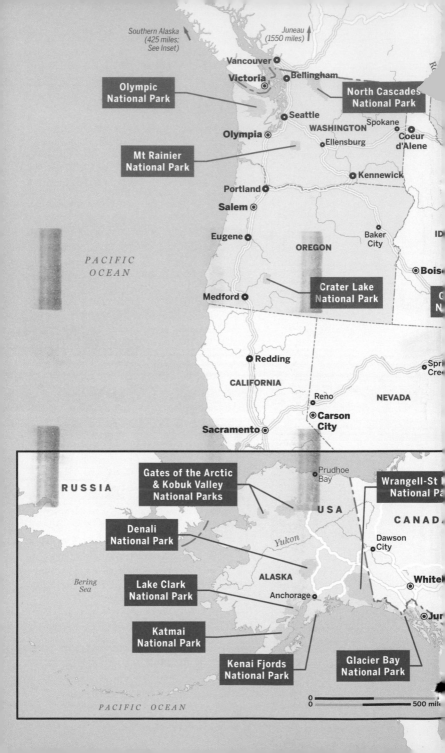

Southern Alaska
(425 miles;
See Inset)

Juneau
(1550 miles)

Vancouver

Victoria

Bellingham

Olympic National Park

North Cascades National Park

Seattle

WASHINGTON

Spokane

Olympia

Ellensburg

Coeur d'Alene

Mt Rainier National Park

Portland

Kennewick

Salem

Eugene

Baker City

OREGON

ID

Boise

PACIFIC OCEAN

Medford

Crater Lake National Park

C N

Redding

Spri Cre

CALIFORNIA

Reno

NEVADA

Carson City

Sacramento

RUSSIA

Gates of the Arctic & Kobuk Valley National Parks

Prudhoe Bay

USA

Wrangell-St National Pa

CANADA

Denali National Park

Yukon

Dawson City

Bering Sea

Lake Clark National Park

Anchorage

ALASKA

White

Katmai National Park

Kenai Fjords National Park

Glacier Bay National Park

Jur

0
0
500 mile

PACIFIC OCEAN

Kenai Fjords National Park (p76)
DAVIDHOFFMANN PHOTOGRAPHY/SHUTTERSTOCK ©

Plan Your Trip

Rocky Mountains & Pacific Northwest's National Parks Top 10

Yellowstone

What makes the world's first national park (p178) so enduring? Geological wonders for one thing, from geysers and fluorescent hot springs to fumaroles and bubbling mud pots. Then there's the wildlife: grizzlies, black bears, wolf packs, elk, bison and moose, roaming across some 3500 sq miles of wilderness. Pitch a tent in Yellowstone's own Grand Canyon (p182), watch wildlife in Lamar Valley, admire the Upper and Lower Falls, wait for Old Faithful to blow and hike through the primeval landscape for a real taste of what is truly the Wild West.

Left: Bison, Yellowstone National Park; Right: Old Faithful Geyser (p178)

Going-to-the-Sun Road, Glacier

Going-to-the-Sun Road (p149) in Glacier National Park offers steely-nerved motorists the drive of their life. Chiseled out of the mountainside and punctuated by some of the sheerest and most vertiginous drop-offs in the US, this 53-mile, vista-laden strip of asphalt offers drivers access to some of the most astounding sights in the Rockies.

Wildlife Watching on Snake River, Grand Teton

Spilling down from Jackson Lake beneath the mighty Teton Range, the wild and scenic Snake River (p154) offers some of the most dramatic mountain scenery in the country. Not only are its waters the perfect place to gawk at the Tetons themselves, but they're prime for wildlife watching. Numerous outfitters offer float trips ranging from gentle to giant water. No matter which you choose, prepare to be awed.

Longs Peak, Rocky Mountain

Whether you hike to the top of its 14,259ft summit or just ogle its glaciated slopes from below, Longs Peak (p172) is truly a feast for the eyes. Given it's the highest peak in the park, it should be. Those who attempt the ascent via the Keyhole Route must first brave the hair-raising Ledges, before conquering the Trough and inching across the Narrows, which finally give way to the (whew!) Homestretch. The views from the top are mind-boggling.

Hoh Rain Forest, Olympic

Embrace the rain! It's what makes this temperate rain forest (p122), in all its Tolkienesque beauty, one of the greenest places in North America. With an average rainfall of up to 170in (that's 14ft), it is also one of the wettest. This tremendous amount of water creates a forest covered in mosses, lichens and ferns, with a canopy so dense the forest floor seems trapped in the perpetual lowlight of dusk. Pack your rain jacket and watch for the Roosevelt elk.

KELLY VANDELLEN/SHUTTERSTOCK ©

JAMES RANDKLEV/GETTY IMAGES ©

Wildflower Season, Mt Rainier

Mt Rainier (p104) gets over 650in of snow annually. It's covered in glaciers, and the high meadows are blanketed in white for nearly nine months of the year. Once the snow finally melts and the meadows are exposed, wildflowers explode into bloom. Avalanche lilies, beargrass, bog orchids, wood nymphs and dozens of other flowers turn the slopes of the Cascades' highest mountain into a rainbow of color.

ALEXANDER S. KUNZ/GETTY IMAGES ©

Crater Lake

Beautiful doesn't even begin to describe Oregon's Crater Lake (p94). It's serene, sublime, transcendent – in other words, it might just blow your mind. A 6-mile-wide caldera created when Mt Mazama erupted nearly 8000 years ago, this amazingly blue lake is filled with some of the purest water you can imagine. It's also America's deepest lake at nearly 2000ft, and so clear you can easily peer 100ft down. Camp, ski or hike in the surrounding old-growth forests while enjoying unforgettable, jaw-dropping views.

Great Sand Dunes

Now here's something special. Colorado's Great Sand Dunes (p164) can feel like a hallucination, with 700ft-high sand dunes rising against a backdrop of the Sangre de Cristo and San Juan mountains. There's lots to do here, whether it's inner tubing, hiking, dune sandboarding or sledding or mountain biking. But most of the time you'll just want to stand and stare at the perfectly sculpted sand ridges and wonder how on earth they got here.

BERNADETTE HEATH/SHUTTERSTOCK ©

Black Canyon of the Gunnison

There's something elemental about the Black Canyon of the Gunnison (p138). Carved by a million-year-old river, this deep canyon ranks among the American West's most astonishing views. And it doesn't matter whether you're peering over the rim or gazing up at the sheer cliffs from the chasm's floor where the sun rarely shines. Hike vertiginous trails, fish this fast-moving river or climb the cliffs.

9

SERGEY YECHIKOV/SHUTTERSTOCK ©

Kayaking, Glacier Bay

Blue-water paddling – kayaking in Alaskan coastal areas, which are characterized by extreme tidal fluctuations, cold water and the possibility of high winds and waves – is the means of escape into areas such as Muir Inlet in Glacier Bay (p62). Everywhere you turn, a tide-water glacier seems to be calving in this grand park, where you may also see humpback whales, black bears, seals and bald eagles.

10

Plan Your Trip
Need to Know

When to Go

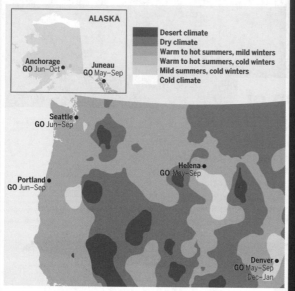

ALASKA

Desert climate
Dry climate
Warm to hot summers, mild winters
Warm to hot summers, cold winters
Mild summers, cold winters
Cold climate

Anchorage
GO Jun–Oct

Juneau
GO May–Sep

Seattle
GO Jun–Sep

Portland
GO Jun–Sep

Helena
GO May–Sep

Denver
GO May–Sep
Dec–Jan

High Season (Jun–early Sep)

o High-country sectors in the Rockies are guaranteed to be open.

o July and August are crowded; reservations are a must.

o June to September can be shoulder season in Colorado.

Shoulder (May–mid-Jun & mid-Sep–Oct)

o Waterfalls in many parks are at their peak in spring.

o High-elevation roads are still closed in spring.

Low Season (mid-Sep–May)

o Cross-country skiing and snowshoeing are excellent in the Rockies.

o Best months for seeing wolves in Yellowstone.

o Expect cooler weather and fewer crowds in many parks.

Entry Fees
Seven-day pass from free to per vehicle/ pedestrian $35/20.

America the Beautiful Annual Pass
$80 per vehicle valid for all national parks for 12 months from purchase. Buy through National Park Service (☎888-275-8747, ext 1; www. nps.gov).

ATMs
Most parks have at least one ATM; widely available in gateway towns.

Credit Cards
Major credit cards widely accepted; Forest Service, BLM and other campgrounds accept cash and/or checks only.

Cell Phones
Coverage inside parks is inconsistent at best.

Wi-fi
Some park lodges have wireless. Outside the parks, most cafes and hotels offer free wireless. Chain hotels sometimes charge.

Tipping
Tip restaurant servers 15% to 20%; porters $2 per bag; hotel maids $2 to $5 per night.

Daily Costs

Budget: Less than $150

- Camping & RV sites: $15–45
- Park entrance fee: free–$35
- Cheap self-catering food or cafe/diner meal $6–15
- Free park shuttles

Midrange: $150–250

- Double room in midrange hotel: $100–250
- Popular restaurant dinner for two: $30–60
- Car hire per day: from $30

Top End: More than $250

- Double room in a top-end hotel: from $200
- Dinner in a top restaurant: $60–100

Advance Planning

Twelve months before Reserve campsites and historic lodge accommodations.
Six months before Reserve hotel rooms in satellite towns if visiting in summer. Book flights.
Three months before Start training if planning to backpack. If you haven't re-served sleeping arrangements, do so.
One month before Secure rental car. Take your own car in for a safety inspection and tune-up if planning a long drive.

Useful Websites

Lonely Planet (www.lonelyplanet.com/usa) Destination information, hotel reviews and more.
National Park Service (NPS; www.nps.gov) Gateway to America's greatest natural treasures, its national parks.

Accommodations

Campsites Reservation and first-come, first-served sites both available in all parks. Flush toilets are common, hot showers are not. Full hookups for RVs usually found outside parks.
Park Lodges Wonderful experience. Usually lack TV; some have wi-fi.
B&Bs Available in gateway towns outside parks; often excellent and usually include wi-fi.
Hotels Occasionally inside parks; most in gateway towns. Nearly all have wi-fi.

Arriving at a National Park

Information Pick up a park newspaper at the entry kiosk and hang onto it; they're packed with useful information.
Camping If you're going for a first-come, first-served site, head straight to the campground. For weekends, try to arrive no later than mid-morning Friday.
Parking People not spending the night inside a park will find parking difficult. Arrive early, park and take free shuttles whenever possible.
Visitor Centers Best places to start exploring the parks. Purchase books and maps, ask rangers questions, check weather reports and trail and road conditions.

Getting Around

Car Most convenient way to travel between the parks. A few park roads are gravel. Traffic inside some parks can be horrendous, especially in summer.

Park Shuttles Many parks have excellent shuttle systems with stops at major visitor sites and trailheads.

Bicycles Some parks have rentals. Good for getting around developed areas. Elsewhere, roads can be steep and shoulders narrow.

Plan Your Trip
Month by Month

January

Strap on your snowshoes or cross-country skis and enjoy the white winter magic in Yellowstone, Glacier and Grand Teton. One of the quieter, greener months in the lowlands and on the coast, where the rains fall.

𝕏 Snowshoeing

Leave the crowds behind and take to the trails of the national parks with snowshoes on your feet. Seeing the high-elevation and northern parks when they're blanketed in snow is a magical experience. Rangers at some of the parks even host guided snowshoe hikes.

𝕏 Truffle Hunting in the Cascades

The Northwest's best native edible truffles are ripe for the picking this month; Eugene becomes a hub with its Oregon Truffle Festival.

Above: Yellowstone National Park (p178)

February

It's the height of ski season. Book ahead for all snow-related activities; resorts and mountain cabins fill up quickly. There are plenty of distractions for those not racing down slopes: wildflowers bloom and whales migrate along the coast.

March

The biting cold of winter fades from the desert parks, and wildflowers begin to bloom at lower elevations. Snow activities are still good at high elevations.

𝕏 Spring Whale-Watching Week

Spot the spring migration of the gray whales anywhere along the Pacific Coast. Around Oregon's Depoe Bay it's semi-organized, with docents and special viewpoints. The northward migration happens through June (www.visittheoregoncoast.com/travel-guides/outdoor-activities/whale-watching/).

April

Wildflowers are in full swing at lower eleva-tions, and waterfalls begin pumping at full force with the beginning of the snowmelt. Even though the rains continue, warmer temperatures and spots of sun inspire more outdoor activities. Easter weekend can be crowded everywhere.

⊙ Spring Wildflowers

Wildflowers put on dazzling springtime dis-plays at the lower-elevation parks. Check the National Park Service websites for wildflower walks, talks and celebrations.

⚚ National Park Week

For an entire week every April, admission to the national parks is free. Early in the year, the US president announces when National Park Week will fall that year. Many of the parks also host free activities.

May

A great time to visit most national parks, although rain is still possible. With children still in school, the masses don't show until the busy Memorial Day weekend, the last weekend of the month.

☆ Sasquatch! Music Festival

Indie-music fans converge on the outdoor Gorge Amphitheater in George, WA, near the Columbia River Gorge, for live music on Memorial Day weekend (www.sasquatch-festival.com).

June

It's still possible to beat the crowds of sum-mer in early June. By late June, the parks are jammed but some passes may be open, rivers are overflowing with snowmelt and mountain wildflowers are blooming.

★ Best Events

Cody Stampede, July

Spring Wildflowers, April

Spring Whale-Watching Week, March

Grand Teton Music Festival, July

Pendleton Round-Up, September

July

High-elevation sectors of the Rockies and Cascades begin opening. It's prime hiking time in the high country, where wildflowers are at their peak. Expect crowds everywhere.

⊙ Cody Stampede

In Yellowstone's gateway communities, ro-deo is the major cultural event of the year. Cowboys take to the saddle throughout June, July and August in various commu-nities. The largest rodeos are the Cody Stampede (www.codystampederodeo. com) and the Wild West Yellowstone Rodeo (www.yellowstonerodeo.com). Note that animal welfare groups often criticize rodeo events as being harmful to animals.

⚚ Independence Day

Across the West, communities celebrate America's birth with rodeos, music festi-vals, barbecues, parades and fireworks on July 4.

⚚ North American Indian Days

In the second week of July, head to the Blackfeet Indian Reservation, immediately east of Glacier National Park, for traditional drumming, dancing and the annual crown-ing of the year's Miss Blackfeet. The four-day festival (www.blackfeetcountry.com) is a wonderful display of Blackfeet traditions.

☉ Summer Wildflowers

There's nothing like hiking through high-country meadows that are blanketed in wildflowers. In high-elevation parks such as Glacier, Rocky Mountain, Yellowstone and Grant Teton, wildflowers bloom intensely during the short growing season between snows.

🎻 Grand Teton Music Festival

Over 40 classical music concerts are held throughout the Jackson Hole region near Grand Teton National Park. Everything from children's concerts to full orchestras are on the menu. Concerts take place almost nightly throughout July and into August. See www.gtmf.org for calendars and to purchase tickets.

August

Hello crowds! It's the height of summer, it's blazing hot, and every hotel and campsite is reserved. First-come, first-served campgrounds are your best bet. Head to the high country, where the weather is superb.

🎻 Christmas in August

Join the Christmas caroling in one of the parks' oddest celebrations, Yellowstone's Christmas in August (celebrated on the 25th). The event dates back to the turn of the last century, when a freak August snowstorm stranded a group of visitors in the Upper Geyser Basin.

September

Summer's last hurrah is the Labor Day holiday weekend. The crowds begin to thin, and by the end of the month things are pretty quiet. If you don't mind brisk evenings, this can be a beautiful time to visit the parks. High-country sectors close by the end of the month.

🎻 Pendleton Round-Up

Country music, dances, art shows, a Native American powwow, bronco-breaking and Western pageantry preside here in Oregon, at one of the country's most famous rodeos. Note that animal welfare groups often criticize rodeo events as being harmful to animals.

October

Fall color is nothing short of fabulous in many of the parks. Crowds are nonexistent and the temperatures are dropping quickly, but shimmering aspens lure road-trippers to Colorado. High-elevation sectors are closed.

November

Winter is creeping in quickly. Most coastal areas, deserts and parks are less busy, with the exception of the Thanksgiving holiday. The ski season begins.

🎿 Yellowstone Ski Festival

This Thanksgiving week celebration at West Yellowstone (www.skirunbikemt.com/yellowstone-ski-festival.html) is a great time for ski buffs and newcomers alike. Highlights include ski clinics and races. Nordic skiing kicks off around this time too.

December

Winter is well under way in most of the parks. High-elevation roads and park sectors are closed, and visitor center and business hours are reduced. Think snowshoeing and cross-country skiing.

🎻 National Audubon Society Christmas Bird Count

Every year around Christmastime, thousands of people take to the wilds to look for and record birds for the Audubon Society's annual survey. Many of the parks organize a count and rely on volunteers to help. Check the National Park Service websites for information.

Plan Your Trip
Get Inspired

Read

Our National Parks (1901) The words of John Muir inspired a nation to embrace national parks.

Ranger Confidential: Living, Working & Dying in the National Parks (2010) Andrea Lankford takes you inside life as a park ranger.

Lost in My Own Backyard (2004) Chuckle your way around Yellowstone with Tim Cahill.

The American Wolf (2017) Nate Blakeslee's masterful story of the wolves of Yellowstone.

Wildlife in America (1959) Peter Matthiessen's classic on America's wildlife story.

American Zion (2019) Betsy Gaines Quammen looks at the intersection of religion and public lands in the American West.

Watch

American Experience: Ansel Adams (2004) Inspire your snapshots with this PBS documentary.

Vacation (1983) Perfect comedy kick-starter for any family vacation.

Into the Wild (2007) Follow Chris McCandless as he kisses his possessions goodbye and hitchhikes to Alaska.

Wild (2014) A recently divorced woman throws caution to the wind to undertake a hike of self-discovery on the Pacific Crest Trail.

The National Parks, America's Best Idea (2009) Ken Burns' 12-hour PBS miniseries is a must.

Listen

Classic Old-Time Fiddle (2007) Perfect fiddle compilation for those long American road trips.

Beautiful Maladies (1998) Nothing spells 'road trip' like a good Tom Waits tune.

This Land is Your Land: The Asch Recordings, Vol. 1 (1997) Woodie Guthrie sings everything from 'This Land is Your Land' to 'The Car Song'.

Anthology of American Folk Music (1952) Dig into the blues, folk and country roots of America with Harry Smith's iconic collection.

Above: Snake River, Grand Teton National Park (p152)

Plan Your Trip
Health & Safety

MAYSKYPHOTO/SHUTTERSTOCK ©

Before You Go

If you require medications bring them in their original, labeled containers. A signed and dated letter from your physician describing your medical conditions and medications, with generic names, is a good idea. If carrying syringes or needles, be sure to have a physician's letter documenting their necessity.

Some of the walks in this book are demanding and most require a reasonable level of fitness. Even if you're tackling the easy or easy–moderate walks, it pays to be relatively fit, rather than launch straight into them after months of sedentary living. If you're aiming for the demanding walks, fitness is essential.

If you have any medical problems, or are concerned about your health, it's a good idea to have a full checkup before you start.

In the Parks

Visiting city dwellers will need to keep their wits about them in order to minimize the chances of suffering an avoidable accident

Above: Yellowstone National Park (p178)

or tragedy. Dress appropriately for the conditions, tell people where you are going, don't try for a big expedition without prior experience, and, above all, respect the wilderness and the inherent dangers that it conceals.

Crime is more common in big cities than in sparsely populated national parks. Nevertheless, use common sense: lock valuables in the trunk of your vehicle, especially if you're parking it at a trailhead overnight, and never leave anything worth stealing in your tent.

Walk Safety – Basic Rules

○ Allow plenty of time to accomplish a walk before dark, particularly when daylight hours are shorter.

○ Study the route carefully before setting out, noting the possible escape routes and the point of no return (where it's quicker to continue than to turn back). Monitor your progress against the time estimated for the walk, and keep an eye on the weather.

○ It's wise not to walk alone. Always leave details of your intended route, the number of people in your group and expected return time with someone responsible before you go, and let that person know when you return.

○ Before setting off, make sure you have a relevant map, compass and whistle, and that you know the weather forecast for the area for the next 24 hours. In the Rockies always carry extra warm, dry layers of clothing and plenty of emergency high-energy food.

Avalanches

Avalanches are a threat during and following storms, in high winds and during temperature changes, particularly when it warms in spring. Educate yourself about the dangers before setting out. Signs of avalanche activity include felled trees and slides.

If you are caught in an avalanche, your chance of survival depends on your ability to keep yourself above the flowing snow and your companions' ability to rescue you. The probability of survival decreases rapidly after half an hour, so the party must be self-equipped, with each member carrying an avalanche beacon, a sectional probe and a collapsible shovel.

Altitude

To prevent acute mountain sickness:

○ Ascend slowly – have frequent rest days, spending two to three nights at each rise of 1000m (3281ft). If you reach a high altitude by trekking, acclimatization takes place gradually and you are less likely to be affected than if you fly directly to high altitude.

○ It is always wise to sleep at a lower altitude than the greatest height reached during the day. Also, once above 3000m (9843ft), care should be taken not to increase the sleeping altitude by more than 300m (984ft) per day.

○ Drink extra fluids. The mountain air is dry and cold and moisture is lost as you

★ Water Purification

To ensure you are getting safe, clean drinking water in the backcountry you have three basic options:

Boiling Water is considered safe to drink if it has been boiled at 100°C for at least a minute. This is best done when you set up your camp and stove in the evening.

Chemical Purification There are two types of chemical additives that will purify water: chlorine and iodine. You can choose from various products on the market. Read the instructions first, be aware of expiration dates and check you are not allergic to either chemical.

Filtration Mobile devices can pump water through microscopic filters and take out potentially harmful organisms. If carrying a filter, take care it doesn't get damaged in transit, read the instructions carefully and always filter the cleanest water you can find.

breathe; evaporation of sweat may occur unnoticed and result in dehydration.

○ Eat light, high-carbohydrate meals for more energy.

○ Avoid alcohol and sedatives.

Rescue & Evacuation

If someone in your group is injured or falls ill and can't move, leave somebody with them while at least one other person goes for help. They should take clear written details of the location and condition of the victim, and of helicopter landing conditions. If there are only two of you, leave the injured person with as much warm clothing, food and water as it's sensible to spare, plus the whistle and torch. Mark the position with something conspicuous – an orange bivvy bag, or perhaps a large stone cross on the ground.

Plan Your Trip
Clothing & Equipment

ALASDAIR TURNER/GETTY IMAGES ©

Deciding what gear is essential for a trip and what will only weigh you down is an art. Smartphone apps, new filtration systems and battery chargers are changing the game. Don't forget essentials, but be ruthless when packing, since every ounce counts when you're lugging your gear up a steep mountain.

Layering

The secret to comfortable walking is to wear several layers of light clothing, which you can easily take off or put on as you warm up or cool down. Most walkers use three main layers: a base layer next to the skin, an insulating layer, and an outer-shell layer for protection from wind, rain and snow.

For the upper body, the base layer is typically a shirt of synthetic material that wicks moisture away from the body and reduces chilling. The insulating layer retains

Above: Forbidden Peak, North Cascades National Park (p116)

heat next to your body, and is usually a (windproof) fleece jacket or sweater. The outer shell consists of a waterproof jacket that also protects against cold wind.

For the lower body, the layers generally consist of either shorts or loose-fitting trousers, thermal underwear ('long johns') and waterproof overtrousers.

When purchasing outdoor clothing, one of the most practical fabrics is merino wool. Though pricier than other materials, natural wool absorbs sweat, retains heat even when wet, and is soft and comfortable to wear. Even better, it doesn't store odors like other sports garments, so you can wear it for several days in a row without inflicting antisocial smells on your tent mates.

Waterproof Shells

Jackets should be made of a breathable, waterproof fabric, with a hood that is roomy enough to cover headwear, but that still allows peripheral vision. Other handy features include underarm zippers for easy ventilation and a large map pocket with a heavy-gauge zipper protected by a storm flap.

Waterproof pants are best with slits for pocket access and long leg zips so that you can pull them on and off over your boots.

Footwear

Running shoes are OK for walks that are graded easy or moderate. However, you'll probably appreciate, if not need, the support and protection provided by hiking boots for more demanding walks. Nonslip soles (such as Vibram) provide the best grip.

Buy boots in warm conditions or go for a walk before trying them on, so that your feet can expand slightly, as they would on a hike. It's also a good idea to carry a pair of sandals to wear at night for getting in and out of tents easily or at rest stops. Sandals are also useful when fording waterways.

Gaiters help to keep your feet dry in wet weather and on boggy ground; they can also deflect small stones or sand and maintain leg warmth. The best are made of strong fabric, with a robust zip protected by a flap, and secure easily around the foot.

Walking socks should be free of ridged seams in the toes and heels.

Backpacks & Daypacks

For day walks, a day pack (30L to 40L) will usually suffice, but for multiday walks you will need a backpack of between 45L and 90L capacity. Even if the manufacturer claims your pack is waterproof, use heavy-duty liners.

Bear Spray

Some of the hikes/activities in the parks take you through bear country. As a last resort, bear spray (pepper spray) has been used effectively to deter aggressive bears, and park authorities often recommend that you equip yourself with a canister when venturing into

backcountry. Be sure to familiarize yourself with the instructions, and only use as a last resort (ie on a charging bear approximately 9m to 15m/30ft to 50ft away from you).

Most shops in or around the parks stock bear spray. Prices typically range from $35 to $45; some places rent it by the day. It is best kept close at hand on a belt around your waist.

Tent

A three-season tent will fulfill most walkers' requirements. The floor and the outer shell, or fly, should have taped or sealed seams and covered zips to stop leaks. The weight can be as low as 2.2lb (1kg) for a stripped-down, low-profile tent, and up to 6.6lb (3kg) for a roomy, luxury, four-season model.

Dome- and tunnel-shaped tents handle windy conditions better than flat-sided tents.

Map & Compass

You should always carry a good map of the area in which you are walking, and know how to read it. Before setting off on your walk, ensure that you are aware of the contour interval, the map symbols, the magnetic declination (difference between true and grid north), plus the main ridge and river systems in the area and the general direction in which you are heading. On the trail, try to identify major landforms such as mountain ranges and valleys, and locate them on your map to familiarize yourself with the geography.

Buy a compass and learn how to use it. The attraction of magnetic north varies in different parts of the world, so compasses need to be balanced accordingly. Compass manufacturers have divided the world into five zones. Make sure your compass is balanced for your destination zone. There are also 'universal' compasses on the market that can be used anywhere in the world.

Plan Your Trip
Rocky Mountains & Pacific Northwest Overview

National Parks

NAME	STATE	ENTRANCE FEE
Black Canyon of the Gunnison National Park (p138)	Colorado	7-day pass per vehicle $20
Crater Lake National Park (p94)	Oregon	7-day pass per vehicle $25
Denali National Park (p44)	Alaska	7-day pass per adult/child $10/free
Gates of the Arctic & Kobuk Valley National Parks (p56)	Alaska	Free
Glacier Bay National Park (p62)	Alaska	Free
Glacier National Park (p140)	Montana	7-day pass per vehicle $35
Grand Teton National Park (p152)	Wyoming	7-day pass per vehicle $35
Great Sand Dunes National Park (p164)	Colorado	7-day pass per vehicle $20
Katmai National Park (p70)	Alaska	Free
Kenai Fjords National Park (p76)	Alaska	Free
Lake Clark National Park (p80)	Alaska	Free
Mt Rainier National Park (p104)	Washington	7-day pass per vehicle $30

DESCRIPTION	GREAT FOR...
No other canyon in America combines the narrow openings, sheer walls and dizzying depths of the Black Canyon.	
The gloriously blue waters of Crater Lake reflect surrounding mountain peaks like a giant dark-blue mirror, making for spectacular photographs and breathtaking panoramas.	
The park is probably your best chance in the Interior (if not in the entire state) of seeing a grizzly bear, moose or caribou.	
These parks are part of a contiguous wilderness harboring no roads and a population of precisely zero.	
Seven tidewater glaciers spill out of the mountains and fill the sea with icebergs of all shapes, sizes and shades of blue.	
Glacier is the only place in the lower 48 states where grizzly bears still roam in abundance, and smart park management has kept the place accessible yet at the same time authentically wild.	
Simply put, this is sublime and crazy terrain, crowned by the dagger-edged Grand Teton (13,770ft).	
Landscapes collide in a shifting sea of sand at Great Sand Dunes National Park, making you wonder whether a spaceship has whisked you to another planet.	
Stand spine-tinglingly close to 1000lb brown bears, who use their formidable power to paw giant salmon out of the river.	
Crowning this park is the massive Harding Ice Field; from it, tidewater glaciers pour down, carving the coast into fjords.	
An awesome array of tundra-covered hills, mountains, glaciers, coastline, the largest lakes in the state and two active volcanoes.	
Mt Rainier (elevation 14,411ft) is the USA's fourth-highest peak (outside Alaska) and arguably its most awe-inspiring	

NAME	STATE	ENTRANCE FEE
North Cascades National Park (p116)	Washington	Free
Olympic National Park (p122)	Washington	7-day pass per vehicle $30
Rocky Mountain National Park (p170)	Colorado	7-day pass per vehicle $35
Wrangell-St Elias National Park (p82)	Alaska	Free
Yellowstone National Park (p178)	Wyoming	7-day pass per vehicle $35

Other NPS-Designated Sites & Areas

NAME	STATE	DESIGNATION
Aleutian Islands WWII National Historic Area (p54)	Alaska	National Historic Area
Iñupiat Heritage Center (p55)	Alaska	New Bedford Whaling National Historical Park
Sitka National Historical Park (p55)	Alaska	National Historical Park

Road Trips

NAME	STATE	DISTANCE/DURATION
Crater Lake Circuit (p98)	Oregon	365 miles / 2-3 days
Mt Rainier Scenic Byways (p108)	Washington	454 miles / 2-3 days
Olympic Peninsula Loop (p128)	Washington	435 miles / 4 days

DESCRIPTION	GREAT FOR...
The lightly trodden North Cascades National Park has no settlements, no overnight accommodations and one unpaved road.	
Home to one of the world's only temperate rainforests, this notoriously wet national park is as 'wild' and 'west' as it gets.	
Rocky Mountain National Park showcases classic alpine scenery, with wildflower meadows and serene mountain lakes set under snowcapped peaks.	
Comprising more than 20,000 sq miles of brawny ice-encrusted mountains, this is the second-largest national park in the world.	
The real showstoppers here are the geysers and hot springs, but at every turn this land of fire and brimstone breathes, belches and bubbles like a giant kettle on the boil.	

DESCRIPTION
In 1996 Congress created this 134-acre national historic site to commemorate the bloody events of WWII that took place on the Aleutian Islands.
This 24,000-sq-ft facility houses a museum, gift shop and a large multipurpose room where short traditional dancing-and-drumming performances take place each afternoon.
This mystical juxtaposition of tall trees and totems is Alaska's smallest national park and the site where the Tlingits were finally defeated by the Russians in 1804.

DESCRIPTION	ESSENTIAL PHOTO
A heavily forested, waterfall-studded loop that takes in serene, mystical Crater Lake, which has some of the clearest, purest water you can imagine.	Oregon's most beautiful body of water, Crater Lake.
Circumnavigate Mt Rainier by car and you'll quickly swap the urban melee of Seattle for forest-covered mountain foothills strafed with huge trees and imbued with Native American myth.	Rainier's snow-topped summit reflected in Reflection Lakes.
Freakishly wet, fantastically green and chillingly remote, the Olympic Peninsula looks like it has been resurrected from a wilder, precivilized era.	Hoh Rain Forest to see greens you've never imagined.

Iceberg Lake, Glacier National Park (p144)

Top Left: Barred owl, Olympic National Park (p122); Top Right: Kenai Fjords National Park (p76);
Above: Yellowstone National Park (p178)

Plan Your Trip
Best Hiking

Above: Chasm Lake, Rocky Mountain National Park (p173); Top Right: Olympic National Park (p122); Bottom Right: Highline Trail, Glacier National Park (p147)

Nothing encapsulates the spirit of the national parks like hiking. Thousands of miles of trails crisscross the parks, offering access to their most scenic mountain passes, highest waterfalls and quietest corners.

Highline Trail, Glacier

The ultimate high country traverse in the shadow of the great continental divide.

Teton Crest Trail, Grand Teton

There's no let-up in the jagged mountain scenery on this 40-mile romp through Wyoming's greatest hits.

Chasm Lake, Rocky Mountain

If you're in good shape, the 8.4-mile round-trip to Chasm Lake is amazing and every bit as beautiful as more-famous Longs Peak.

Enchanted Valley Trail, Olympic

Magnificent mountain views, roaming wildlife and lush rainforests – all on a 13-mile out-and-back trail.

Cascade Pass Trail, North Cascades

High-altitude scenery at its best in the lightly trodden Pacific Northwest wilderness.

Plan Your Trip
Best Wildlife Watching

Above: Wolf, Yellowstone National Park (p178); Top Right: Moose, Grand Teton National Park (p152); Bottom Right: Grizzly bear, Glacier National Park (p140)

North America is home to creatures both great and small and the national parks of the Rockies and the Pacific Northwest are among the best places to see them.

Yellowstone

Go looking for wolves, bison, grizzlies and more in Yellowstone, more than ever one of the best wildlife parks in America.

Oxbow Bend, Grand Teton

Moose, elk, bald eagles, trumpeter swans, blue herons and more can be seen at this special place in Grand Teton.

Glacier

Your best chance of seeing a grizzly in the lower 48, as well as 70 other mammals including cougars and wolverines.

Rocky Mountain National Park

The extravagantly horned bighorn sheep is one of the grand wildlife sights of the American West.

North Cascades

Bald eagles and ospreys circle high above this wilderness. At ground level there's black bear, wolverine, river otter, mountain lion and bobcat.

Pacific Northwest Coast

Scan the seas for orcas, sea lions, leopard-spotted harbor seals and (from November to December and April to May) gray and humpback whales.

Plan Your Trip
Best Family Experiences

Above: Hoh Rain Forest, Olympic National Park (p122); Top Right: Great Sand Dunes National Park (p164); Bottom Right: Black Canyon of the Gunnison National Park (p138)

There's something inherently gratifying about bringing kids to a national park, most of which offer educational programs and activities designed to engage children in the environments around them.

Sand Sledding, Great Sand Dunes

Landscapes collide here in a shifting sea of sand – you might wonder whether a spaceship has whisked you to another planet.

Hoh Rain Forest, Olympic Peninsula

Enter a hobbit-like world of huge mossy trees and giant dripping ferns, and let your imagination run wild in this very old and very wet rainforest.

Rafting, North Cascades

The tranquil Upper Skagit is an ideal destination for family rafting fun with Class II or III routes through soulful old-growth forest filled with wildlife.

Yellowstone

If you want your child to fall in love with the wild, take them to Yellowstone, which has everything from bison and wolves to grizzlies and geysers.

Black Canyon of the Gunnison

Landscapes that seem to spring from a child's imagination, and the kind of place where geology seems very much alive.

Plan Your Trip
Best Adventures

Above: Skiing in Grand Teton National Park (p152); Top Right: Mt Rainier National Park (p104); Bottom Right: Hiking in North Cascades National Park (p116)

With environments ranging from the Great Plains to the glacial snowfields of the Pacific Northwest, the national parks of the Rockies and Pacific Northwest have no shortage of spectacular settings for a bit of adventure.

Mountaineering, Mt Rainier

The snowcapped summit and forest-covered foothills boast numerous hiking trails, huge swaths of flower-carpeted meadows, and an alluring conical peak that presents a formidable challenge for aspiring climbers.

Nordic Skiing & Snowshoeing, Grand Teton

Enjoy some winter fun when the crowds have gone home in Wyoming from hair-raising ski-mountaineering on Grand Teton to groomed x-country trails in the foothills.

Great Northern Traverse, Glacier

A 58-mile haul that cuts through the heart of grizzly country and crosses the Continental Divide.

Hiking the Backcountry, North Cascades

Hiking trails for the serious hiker take you through a world of forests, glaciers, mountains, wildflowers and ruggedly beautiful backcountry.

Cross-Country Skiing, Mt Rainier

Ski the back trails around Mt Rainier and you'll feel like a frontier pioneer far from the world and its noise.

Plan Your Trip
Best Views

Above: Mormon Row, Grand Teton National Park (p158); Top Right: Going-to-the-Sun Rd, Glacier National Park (p149); Bottom Right: Wizard Island, Crater Lake National Park (p100)

With so much all-round geological drama happening, it should come as no surprise that the parks of the Rockies and Pacific Northwest offer some of America's most spectacular views.

Going-to-the-Sun Road, Glacier

Nowhere in the American West does the intersection between the Rockies and the Great Plains, two iconic US landforms, come together in one such awe-inspiring view.

Black Canyon of the Gunnison

Look over the rim of the canyon and down into the 2000ft-deep abyss if you dare. Your head will spin, but you'll do it again.

Longs Peak, Rocky Mountain

Both from the 14,259ft summit reached via a serious climb or from down below, this is one of the prettiest panoramas anywhere in the Rockies.

Mormon Row, Grand Teton

Aged wooden barns and fence rails framed by the superb Tetons make this one of the signature viewpoints out West.

Mt Washburn, Yellowstone

From Dunraven Pass, the wildflower-lined Mt Washburn Trail climbs 3 miles to expansive views from the summit of Mt Washburn (10,243ft).

Crater Lake

Any way you look at it, Oregon's Crater Lake will blow your mind: it's America's deepest lake with transparent waters in a perfectly formed volcanic caldera.

ALASKA

In This Chapter

Alaska

There's nowhere in America quite like Alaska. A place apart geographically (Alaska lies 1500 miles north of the lower 48), this wild and beautiful land is American for wilderness. Except for isolated pockets of human population, Alaska is nature in the ascendancy, a state whose eight national parks cover 54 million acres and enclose within their boundaries Arctic realms of astonishing beauty. Whether it's landscapes, wildlife, or that intangible sense of feeling somewhere beyond the end of the paved road, Alaska has it in abundance.

Don't Miss

● Cycling or bussing Denali's long and winding Park Road (p44)

● Paddling an icy wilderness amid the icebergs in Glacier Bay (p62)

● Watching grizzlies catch the salmon at Brooks Camp in Katmai (p70)

● Looking for orcas and listening to the thundering of glaciers in Kenai Fjords (p76)

● Hiking the silent backcountry of Gates of the Arctic (p56)

When to Go

Summer (June to August) is easily the best time to go. It begins in June with solstice festivals and 20-hour days, and crescendos in July and August with salmon runs and snow-free trails.

Getting around is more difficult in May and September, but there are trade-offs: the northern lights usually appear in late September. Southeast Alaska is sunny during May, but rainy in September and October.

Winter is complicated, and temperatures plummet from October to April. Longer, warmer days make late February best for winter sports, but some tour companies close for winter.

Previous page: Denali National Park (p44)

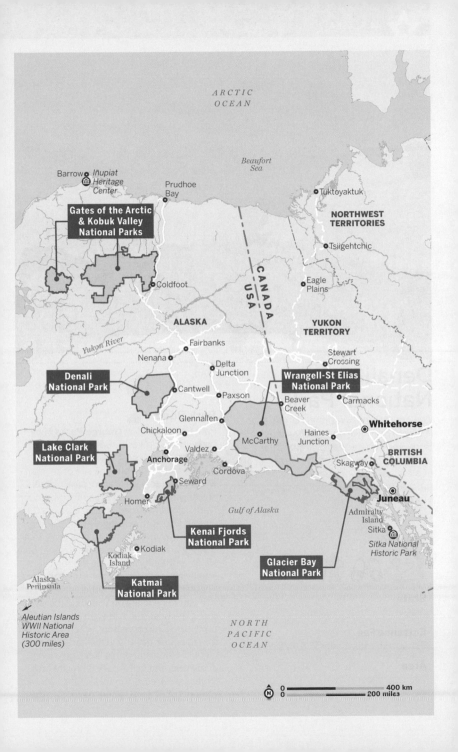

ARCTIC
OCEAN

Beaufort
Sea

Barrow○ ○ Iñupiat
Heritage
Center

○ Prudhoe
Bay

○ Tuktoyaktuk

**NORTHWEST
TERRITORIES**

**Gates of the Arctic
& Kobuk Valley
National Parks**

○ Tsiigehtchic

C
A
N
A
D
A

U
S
A

○ Coldfoot

○ Eagle
Plains

ALASKA

**YUKON
TERRITORY**

Yukon River

○ Fairbanks

○ Stewart
Crossing

○ Nenana

○ Delta
Junction

**Denali
National Park**

○ Cantwell

○ Paxson

○ Carmacks

**Wrangell-St Elias
National Park**

○ Beaver
Creek

○ Glennallen

○ Chickaloon

○ McCarthy

○ Haines
Junction

◎ **Whitehorse**

**Lake Clark
National Park**

○ Valdez

Anchorage

○ Cordova

**BRITISH
COLUMBIA**

○ Seward

○ Skagway

○ Homer

Gulf of Alaska

◎ **Juneau**

**Kenai Fjords
National Park**

Admiralty
Island

○ Kodiak

Sitka ○

**Glacier Bay
National Park**

Sitka National
Historic Park

Kodiak
Island

Alaska
Peninsula

**Katmai
National Park**

NORTH
PACIFIC
OCEAN

Aleutian Islands
WWII National
Historic Area
(300 miles)

N
0 ──── 400 km
0 ──── 200 miles

George Parks Hwy

Denali National Park

The joy of Denali National Park is that it's both primeval and easily accessible. Here, you can peer at a grizzly bear, moose or caribou from the comfort of a bus, or trek into 6 million acres of tundra, boreal forest and ice-capped mountains.

Great For...

State
Alaska

Entrance Fee
7-day pass adult/under 15 $10/free

Area
9492 sq miles

Park Road

Park Road begins at **George Parks Hwy** and winds 92 miles through the heart of the park, ending at Kantishna, an old mining settlement and the site of several wilderness lodges. Early on, park officials envisaged the onset of bumper-to-bumper traffic along this road and wisely closed almost all of it to private vehicles. During the summer, motorists can only drive to a parking area along the Savage River at Mile 15. To venture further along the road you must walk, cycle, be part of a tour or, most popularly, take a park shuttle or tour bus.

If you're planning on spending the day riding the buses (it's an eight-hour round-trip to the Eielson Visitor Center (p52), the most popular day trip in the park), pack plenty of food and drink. It can be a long, dusty ride, and in the park there are only limited services at the Toklat River Contact Station (p52) and Eielson Visitor Center.

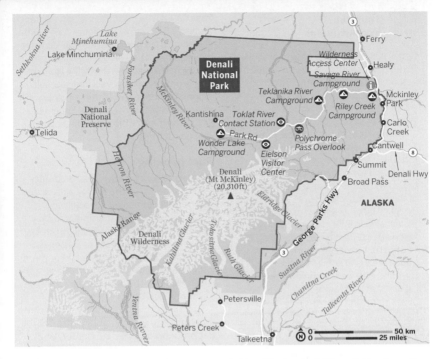

Carry a park map so you know where you are and can scope out ridges or riverbeds that appeal for hiking.

Wildlife Watching

Because hunting has never been allowed in the park, professional photographers refer to animals in Denali as 'approachable wildlife.' That means bear, moose, Dall sheep and caribou aren't as skittish here as in other regions of the state. For this reason, and because Park Rd was built to maximize the chances of seeing wildlife by traversing high open ground, the park is an excellent place to view a variety of animals.

On board the park shuttle buses, your fellow passengers will be armed with binoculars and cameras to help scour the terrain for animals, most of which are so accustomed to the rambling buses that they rarely run and hide. When someone spots something and yells 'Stop!', the driver will pull over for viewing and picture

taking. The best wildlife watching is on the first morning bus.

Day Hiking

Even for those who have neither the desire nor the equipment for an overnight trek, hiking is the best way to enjoy the park and see the land and its wildlife. You can hike virtually anywhere that hasn't been closed to prevent an impact on wildlife.

For a day hike (which doesn't require a permit), ride the shuttle bus and get off at any valley, riverbed or ridge that grabs your fancy. Check in at the Backcountry Information Center (p52) or Denali Bus Depot for suggestions.

Here's an important reminder for shuttle bus riders: while you can hop on any shuttle bus heading back to the park gates, those buses are often packed. It's generally easier to get yourself on a bus if you try to board at a recognized bus stop, such as Toklat River (p52) **Polychrome**

Tour Bus vs Shuttle Bus

Denali National Park is traversed by Park Rd, which is closed to car traffic at Mile 15 during the summer season. Past here, visitors must come in on either a tour bus or a shuttle bus. Which should you opt for?

Tour buses offer a narrated, pre-scribed park experience. They're comfortable, more expensive than shuttle buses, and aimed at older travelers and those who will not be able to hike inside of the park. Narrated tours include a packed lunch. See www.nps.gov/dena for more information and www.reservedenali.com for reservations.

Shuttle buses are ostensibly just that: a means of going into and out of the park, with no accompanying narration. That said, we've ridden shuttle buses with chatty drivers who have been happy to point out wildlife and provide commentary. Shuttle buses are converted school buses, so they're not particularly comfortable (although they're not uncomfortable either). They're cheaper than tour buses, and you can hop on and off to hike.

In general, we recommend shuttle buses for independent travelers who want to explore the park at their own pace. If you don't want to hike, a tour bus may be the better option.

If you take the shuttle bus, where should you get off? You buy your shuttle ticket to a certain destination within the park; while you can ride the bus back from anywhere, your ticket only allows you to proceed, via bus, up to a certain point within Denali. So how far in should you go?

The answer is entirely up to you, but most shuttle bus passengers disembark at the Eielson Visitor Center (p52), which is a good way inside the park. Getting off at Eielson gives you a good taste of park landscape, but also gives you some free time to hike before heading back toward the entrance.

Pass (Mile 46, Park Rd), the Eielson Visitor Center (p52), etc, where your name will be placed on a list and park staff will do what they can to get you on board. While many people flag a bus down from the road on a daily basis, you may well find yourself waiting for hours in cold rain for a bus with an empty seat. Obviously, the larger your group, the greater the risk of finding a bus with no room.

Backpacking

The park is divided into 87 backcountry units, and for 41 of these only a regulated number of backpackers (usually four to six) are allowed in at a time. You may spend a maximum of seven nights in any one unit, and a maximum of 30 consecutive nights in the backcountry. For more information download a *Denali Backpacking Guide* from the national park's website (www.nps.gov/dena).

Permits are needed if you want to camp overnight and you can obtain these at the Backcountry Information Center (p52), where you'll also find wall maps with the unit outlines and a quota board indicating the number of vacancies in each. Permits are issued only a day in advance, and the most popular units fill up fast. It pays to be flexible: decide which areas you're aiming for, and be prepared to take any zone that's open. If you're picky, you might have to wait several days.

After you've decided where to go, the next step is to watch the required backcountry orientation video, followed by a brief safety talk that covers, among other things, proper use of the bear-proof food containers you'll receive free of charge with your permit. The containers are bulky, but they work – they've reduced bear encounters dramatically since 1986. It's also worth noting that you're required to carry out dirty toilet paper (you bury your waste), so be sure to take at least a dozen ziplock bags. Finally, after receiving your permit, buy the topographic maps ($8) for your unit and head over to the Wilderness Access Center (p52) to purchase a ticket for a camper bus ($40) to take you to the starting point of your hike.

For an overview of the different units in the park, check out the park's website for the brilliant *Backcountry Camping and Hiking Guide*. Its unit-by-unit descriptions include access points, possible hiking corridors, dangers and, maybe best of all, pictures from the area.

Cycling

No special permit is needed to cycle on Park Rd, but cycling off-road is prohibited. Camper buses and some shuttle buses will carry bicycles, but only two at a time and only if you have a reservation. Many cyclists ride the bus in and cycle back out, carrying their gear and staying at campsites they've reserved along the way. It's also possible to take an early-morning bus in, ride for several hours and catch a bus back the same day. The highest point on the road is Highway Pass (3980ft). The entrance area is at 1585ft. Note that Park Rd is narrow, but buses are used to

cyclists, and drivers generally do a grand job of giving riders a decent berth.

River Rafting

Thanks to Denali tourists, the Nenana River is the most popular white-water-rafting area in Alaska. The river's main white-water stretch begins near the park entrance and ends 10 miles north, near Healy. It's rated class III and IV, and involves standing waves, rapids and holes with names such as 'Coffee Grinder' in sheer-sided canyons. South of the park entrance, the river is much milder, but to many it's just as interesting as it veers away from both the highway and the railroad, increasing your chances of sighting wildlife.

Rafting companies offer similar guided trips on both stretches, in which either the guide does all the work or you help paddle. Advance reservations (no deposit) are accepted, and all trips include dry suits and shuttle pick-ups. The canyon and the easier 'wilderness' paddles go for about $99, and last around three hours.

Moose in Denali

A Mountain by Any Other Name

The Athabascans called it Denali or the 'Great One.' Their brethren to the south in the Susitna Valley called it Doleika, the 'Big Mountain.' The Aleuts meanwhile referred to it as Traleika. The first European to spot the peak, George Vancouver, didn't bother to call it anything, while Ferdinand von Wrangell, a prominent Russian administrator in the 19th century, wrote 'Tenada' on his maps. So why was North America's highest peak called McKinley for over a century?

During the gold-rush days, the mountain was known locally as Densmore's Mountain, in honor of a local prospector. But soon it was dubbed Mt McKinley for William McKinley, an Ohioan who later became president of the United States. McKinley ran for office against a politician who wanted to use silver instead of gold as the backing standard for American currency, but McKinley was a strong defender of the gold standard. A man named William Dickey, a gold miner, named the mountain in order to flip the bird at rival silver miners.

In 1975, the state of Alaska, via its Board of Geographic Names, changed the name of the mountain to Denali, and sent an official request to Washington, DC, asking for the nation to do the same. That authority is vested in the United States Board on Geographic Names, but the agency had its hands tied by Ohio Congress members and senators (remember, William McKinley was from Ohio), who apparently thought the federal government was slacking when it came to insulting Native Americans.

This impasse continued until 2015, when then president Barack Obama ordered his Secretary of the Interior, Sally Jewell, to rename the mountain.

Scaling the Mountain

So, has gazing at lordly Mt McKinley – sorry, Denali – from the seat of an aircraft infected you with summit fever?

Denali's storied mountaineering history adds considerably to the mythic business of scaling the peak. Between 1200 and 1300 climbers attempt it each year, spending an average of three weeks on the slopes. About 80% use the West Buttress route, which involves flying in a ski plane from Talkeetna to the 7200ft Kahiltna Glacier and from there climbing for the South Peak, passing a medical/rescue camp maintained by mountaineering clubs and the National Park Service (NPS) at 14,220ft.

Top: Savage River; Bottom: Wonder Lake campground

In a good season (April through July), when storms are not constantly sweeping across the range, more than 50% of expeditions will be successful. In a bad year, that rate falls below 40%, and several climbers may die. Particularly grim was the annus horribilis of 1991, when 11 lives were lost.

If you're a seasoned alpinist you can mount an expedition yourself, or be among the 25% of Denali climbers who are part of guided ascents. If you're looking for a local guiding company, try **Alaska Mountaineering School** (☑907-733-1016; www.climb alaska.org), which charges $8900 to lead you up the mountain. Another acclaimed company with a high success rate is Seattle-based **Alpine Ascents** (☑206-378-1927; www. alpineascents.com). Its trips start at $8600 excluding meals, lodging and flights to Alaska. Book at least a year in advance.

Campground Programs
Rangers present 30- to 45-minute nightly talks on Denali's wildlife and natural history at the park's campgrounds – Riley Creek (p52), **Savage River** (www.nps.gov/ dena; Mile 14, Park Rd; campsites $24-30) ✿, **Teklanika River** (Mile 29, Park Rd; campsites $25) ✿ and **Wonder Lake** (Mile 85, Park Rd; tent sites $16) ✿. You're welcome to show up even if you're not camping. The talks are at 7:30pm nightly; call ☑907-683-9532 or visit www.nps.gov/dena/planyourvisit for more information. Talks begin on June 8 at Wonder Lake, and in mid-May at the other campgrounds; all talks end around mid-September.

Lectures are also offered in the amphitheater at **McKinley Chalet Resort** (☑907-683-6450; www.westmarkhotels.com/ destinations/denali-hotel; Mile 238.9, George Parks Hwy; ☼10am Mon, 3:30pm Tue-Sat) FREE.

Essential Information

Consider making reservations at least six months in advance for a park campsite during the height of summer, and at least three months ahead for accommodations outside the park. The park entrance fee is $10 per person, good for seven days.

There's only one road through the park: the 92-mile unpaved Park Rd, which is closed to private vehicles after Mile 15 in summer. Shuttle buses run from the middle of May until September past Mile 15. Sometimes, if the snow melts early in April, visitors will be allowed to proceed as far as Mile 30 until the shuttle buses begin operation. The park entrance area, where most visitors congregate, extends a scant 4 miles up Park Rd. It's here you'll find the park headquarters, visitor center and main campground, as well as the **Wilderness Access Center** (WAC; ☑907-683-9532; Mile 0.5, Park Rd; ☺5am-7pm late May–mid-Sep), where you pay your park entrance fee and arrange campsites and shuttle-bus bookings to take you further into the park. Across the lot from the WAC sits the **Backcountry Information Center** (BIC; ☑907-683-9532; ☺9am-6pm late May–mid-Sep), where backpackers get backcountry permits and bear-proof food containers.

There are few places to stay within the park, excluding campgrounds, and only one restaurant. Most visitors base themselves in the nearby communities of Cantwell, McKinley Park, Carlo Creek and Healy.

When to Come

From May 15 to June 1, park services are just starting up and access to the backcountry is limited. Visitor numbers are low but shuttle buses only run as far as **Toklat River** (Mile 53, Park Rd; ☺9am-7pm late May–mid-Sep) ✿ **FREE**. From June 1 to 8, access increases and the shuttle buses run as far as **Eielson Visitor Center** (☑907-683-9532; www.nps.gov/dena/planyourvisit/the-eielson-visitor-center.htm; Mile 66, Park Rd; ☺9am-5:30pm early Jun-mid Sep) **FREE**. After June 8, the park is in full swing till late August.

Shuttle buses stop running after the second Thursday after Labor Day in September. Following a few days in which lottery winners are allowed to take their private vehicles further, the road closes to all traffic until the following May.

While most area lodges close, **Riley Creek Campground** (www.nps.gov/dena; Mile 0.25, Park Rd; tent sites $24, RV sites $24-30) ✿ stays open in winter and camping is free, though the water and sewage facilities don't operate. If you have the equipment, you can use the unplowed Park Rd and the rest of the park for cross-country skiing, snowshoeing or dogsledding.

Reservations

From December 1 you can reserve campsites and shuttle buses online for the following summer tourist season through the **Denali National Park Reservation Service** (☑800-622-7275; www.reservedenali.com) operated by Aramark.

Note that sites in the Sanctuary River and Igloo Creek campgrounds can only be reserved in person at the WAC two days in advance, and backcountry permits one day in advance.

Sleeping

You should definitely reserve something in midsummer – even if it's just a campsite – before showing up. Note the Denali Borough charges a 7% accommodations tax on top of listed prices. High-end accommodations in and around the park generally feels overpriced.

Canyon is as close as the Denali area comes to a 'village.' In essence, it's a convenient service center consisting of a thin strip of wooden shops, accommodations, gas stations and stores clustered either side of the George Parks Hwy, roughly a mile north of the park entrance area (a walking path links the two). The western side of the road is dominated by two cruise-line-owned hotels. The eastern side harbors a skinny line of shops, restaurants and outdoor-adventure specialists. ∎

Top left: Wilderness Access Center; Top right: Toklat River; Bottom: Eielson Visitor Center

Alaska's Historical Monuments

Few people travel to Alaska for historical enlightenment, yet the state harbors plenty of echoes from a past clouded by battles, WWII bombings and late-19th-century gold rushes.

Chilkoot Trail

The Chilkoot Trail, the epic trek undertaken by over 30,000 gold-rush stampeders in 1897–98, is sometimes known as the 'Meanest 33 Miles in America.' Its appeal is legendary and, consequently, more than 3000 people spend three to five days following the historic route between Skagway (Alaska) and Lake Bennett (Canada) every summer.

Aleutian Islands WWII National Historic Area, Unalaska

In 1996 Congress created this 134-acre national historic site to commemorate the bloody events of WWII that took place on the Aleutian Islands. To learn about the 'Forgotten War,' begin at the Aleutian Islands WWII Visitor Center, near the airport, in the original air-control tower built in 1942.

Sitka National Historical Park

This mystical juxtaposition of tall trees and totems is Alaska's smallest national park and the site where the Tlingits were finally defeated by the Russians in 1804. The mile-long Totem Trail winds its way past 18 totems first displayed at the 1904 Louisiana Exposition in St Louis, MO, and then moved to the park.

Iñupiat Heritage Center

This 24,000-sq-ft facility houses a museum, gift shop and a large multipurpose room where short traditional dancing-and-drumming performances take place each afternoon. Local crafts-people often assemble in the lobby to sell masks, whalebone carvings and fur garments and are happy to talk about their craft and techniques.

DESIGN PICS INC/ALAMY STOCK PHOTO ©

Caribou, Kobuk Valley National Park

Gates of the Arctic & Kobuk Valley National Parks

With no roads, no cell-phone coverage and a population of precisely zero, Gates of the Arctic National Park is a wilderness virtually unchanged in four millenia. The dunes of Kobuk Valley National Park, to its southwest, have a surreal, severe beauty.

Great For...

State
Alaska

Entrance Fee
Free

Area
13,238 sq miles (Gates of the Arctic)
2805 sq miles (Kobuk Valley)

You don't come to these remote Alaskan parks to stroll along interpretive boardwalks, or even follow something as rudimentary as a trail (there aren't any). Tackled alone, this is a land for brave travelers with advanced outdoor experience, plenty of time on their hands and a flexible budget (read: it's costly). Alternatively, you can sign up with one of a handful of agencies and go on a guided backcountry or flightseeing tour.

Gates of the Arctic is the more accessible park as it starts just 5 miles west of the Dalton Hwy, meaning you can technically hike in, although charter flights out of Coldfoot and Bettles are more common. Kobuk Valley is reached via charters out of the small settlement of Kotzebue.

Hiking

Most backpackers enter the parks by way of charter air-taxis, which can land on lakes, rivers or river bars. Once on the ground,

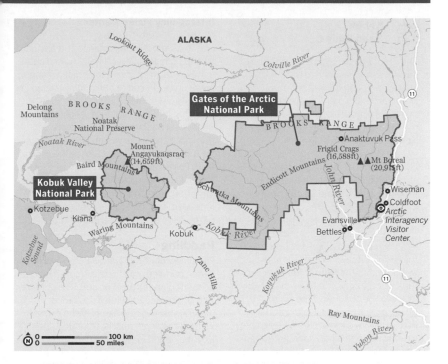

Kobuk Sand Dunes

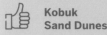

Kobuk Sand Dunes

The great Alaskan wilderness encompasses almost every ecosystem your imagination can devise, but admit it: you probably didn't think 'sand dunes' when someone brought up the 49th state. But they're here in **Kobuk Valley National Park** (☑907-442-3890; www.nps.gov/kova) – some 20,500 acres of rolling sand, the largest collection of dunes in Arctic North America, a landscape so otherworldly it's been used by NASA as an analog for the environment on Mars.

There's not just sand dunes at this park, located 25 miles above the Arctic Circle. You'll also find the watershed of the **Kobuk River**, which runs through a dramatically beautiful valley in the shadow of the Baird Mountains. But you have to get here first, and that's the trick. There are no roads into this park, and no trails inside of it – Kobuk is expensive to access, and visitors must possess a high level of wilderness savvy.

they often follow the long, open valleys for extended treks or work their way to higher elevations where open tundra provides good hiking terrain.

While this appears to make planning an impossibly vague task, the landscape limits the areas that aircraft can land or pick you up, as well as where you can hike. Park staff suggest consulting flight and guide companies, as well as topographic maps, for possible routes and then running it by them to make sure the area is not overused. If it is, they can suggest alternatives.

The only treks that don't require chartering a plane are those in Gates of the Arctic beginning from the Dalton Hwy (near Wiseman), or from the village of Anaktuvuk Pass. For hikes from the highway, which lead into several different areas along the eastern side of the park, stop at the **Arctic**

Interagency Visitor Center (☑907-678-5209; CentralYukon@blm.gov; ⊙11am-10pm Jun-Aug) in Coldfoot for assistance and advice on trip planning. Several well-known routes in this area are showing too much wear and are even beginning to affect the livelihood of subsistence hunters.

Hiking into the park from Anaktuvuk Pass is surprisingly one of the more economical options, as you only need to pay for a regular scheduled flight to the village from Fairbanks. From the airstrip it's just a few miles' hike to the northern edge of the park. You can camp for free by the airstrip if needed, but until you enter the park get permission to camp elsewhere.

Paddling

For a view of Kobuk National Park from the water, paddlers can try the Salmon River, protected under the Wild and Scenic Rivers Act, or the slow-moving Kobuk River.

Floatable rivers in Gates of the Arctic include the John, Alatna, Noatak, Kobuk, Koyukuk and Tinayguk.

The waterways range in difficulty from class I to III, and you should consult the park or guide companies about possible routes.

Canoes can be rented in Bettles at **Bettles Lodge** (☑907-692-5111; www.bettleslodge.com; tour packages incl accommodation per person s/d $890/1020, plus $250/275 each additional night) for around $270 per week.

Flightseeing

The approved air-taxi services that operate to the national parks also generally run flightseeing tours, from which you can snap excellent pictures of the Kobuk Valley watershed and caribou herds.

Guided Trips

The tour operator **Arctic Wild** (☑907-479-8203; www.arcticwild.com) can put together guided backpacking or canoeing trips of various lengths into the parks, including expeditions aimed at spotting the Western Arctic caribou herd, the largest caribou herd in the country. Trips run in August.

Arctic Interagency Visitor Center

Essential Information

Getting There & Away

Gateway towns are reached from Anchorage and Fairbanks via commercial airline.

The most common way to enter Kobuk Valley is via park-approved air taxis and tour operators. In summer, some visitors enter by boat on the Kobuk River after being dropped off at indigenous villages by bush plane.

Bettles offers meals, lodging and air transport into Gates of the Arctic backcountry. Other visitors fly in from Coldfoot on the Dalton Hwy, or hike in directly from Wiseman, just north of Coldfoot. To the north, the remote Alaska Native village of Anaktuvuk Pass is another access point if traveling by foot. Contact the Anaktuvuk Ranger Station for more information on visiting from here.

The park is accessible via snowmachine through winter.

Visitor Information

The park is open year-round. There is a visitor center in Kotzebue within the **Northwest Arctic Heritage Center** (🕑9am-6pm Mon-Sat, Jun-Sep, Mon-Fri Oct-May). **Anaktuvuk Ranger Station** (🗗907-661-3520; www.nps.gov/gaar; 🕑8am-5pm Jun-Sep) can help you plan your trip from Anaktuvuk. In Bettles, **Bettles Ranger Station & Visitor Center** (🗗907-692-5495; www.nps.gov/gaar; 🕑8am-5pm Jun-Sep) is in a log building less than a quarter mile from the airstrip.

Summer temperatures can climb to 100°F, yet freezing conditions and snow can occur anytime. There is private land within the park; avoid areas clearly marked as such.

Independent travelers do not require permits, but organized groups do – contact the park at 🗗907-442-3890. Independent visitors must be completely self-sufficient; there are no facilities in the park.

The **Morris Thompson Cultural & Visitors Center** (🗗907-459-3700; www.morristhompsoncenter.org; 🕑8am-9pm late May-early Sep, to 5pm mid-Sep–mid-May) in Fairbanks has a parks desk that dispenses good information on NPS destinations in Alaska. ∎

Kobuk River

Humpback whale

Glacier Bay National Park

Glacier Bay is the crowning jewel of the cruise-ship industry and a dreamy destination for anybody who has ever paddled a kayak. Seven tidewater glaciers spill out of the mountains and fill the sea with icebergs of all shapes, sizes and shades of blue, making this an icy wilderness renowned worldwide.

Great For...

State
Alaska

Entrance Fee
Free

Area
5220 sq miles

Apart from its high concentration of tidewater glaciers, Glacier Bay is a dynamic habitat for humpback whales. Other wildlife seen at Glacier Bay includes porpoises, sea otters, brown and black bears, wolves, moose and mountain goats.

The park is an expensive side trip, even by Alaskan standards. Plan on spending at least $400 for a trip from Juneau. Of the 500,000 annual visitors, more than 95% arrive aboard a ship and never leave it. The rest are a mixture of tour-group members, who head straight for the lodge, and backpackers, who gravitate toward the free campground.

❶ Glacier Bay

This bay offers an excellent opportunity for people who have some experience on the water but not necessarily as kayakers, because a tour boat run by Glacier Bay Lodge & Tours (p67), drops off and

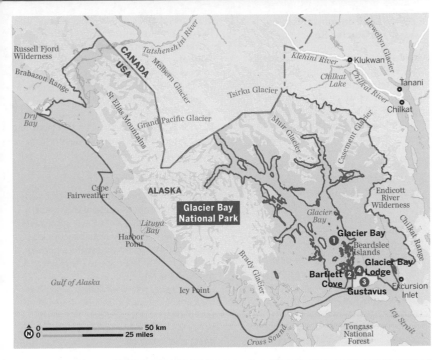

Kayaking in Glacier Bay

Environmental Issues in Glacier Bay

Glacier Bay has seen several disputes between the cruise-ship industry and environmentalists. After the number of whales seen in the park dropped dramatically in 1978, the NPS reduced ship visits during the three-month season. But the cruise-ship industry lobbied the US Congress and the NPS in 1996 to approve a 30% increase in vessels allowed in the bay. Environmentalists sued, and eventually a compromise of two large cruise ships per day was hammered out.

But the whales aren't the only area of concern here. Glacier Bay's ice, like glaciers all over Alaska, is rapidly melting. This is particularly true in Muir Inlet, or the East Arm as it's commonly called. Twenty years ago it was home to three active tidewater glaciers, but now there is only one, McBride. Only two glaciers in the park are advancing; Johns Hopkins and Margerie. The rest are receding and thinning.

picks up paddlers at two spots, usually at the entrance of the Muir Inlet (East Arm) and inside the West Arm. By using the tour boat, you can skip the long and open paddle up the bay and enjoy only the well-protected arms and inlets where the glaciers are located. The most dramatic glaciers are in the West Arm, but either one will require at least four days to paddle to glaciers if you are dropped off *and* picked up. With only a drop-off, you need a week to 10 days to paddle from either arm back to Bartlett Cove.

Paddlers who want to avoid the tour-boat fares but still long for a kayak adventure should try the **Beardslee Islands**. While there are no glaciers to view, the islands are a day's paddle from Bartlett Cove and offer calm water, protected channels and pleasant beach camping. Wildlife includes black bears, seals and bald eagles, and the tidal pools burst with activity at low tide.

Alaska Mountain Guides & Climbing School (☎800-766-3396; www.alaskamoun tainguides.com) runs several guided kayak trips into Glacier Bay. A seven-day paddle to the West Arm, which includes tour transportation as well as all equipment and food, is $2950 per person, and an eight-day paddle up the East Arm that begins from Bartlett Cove is $2950.

❷ Bartlett Cove

Bartlett Cove is home to the national park headquarters and the site of the visitor center (p68) and Glacier Bay Lodge (p67). This is where the ferry from Juneau ties up, paddlers rent kayaks and visitors hop on the tour boat for a cruise to the glaciers 40 miles up the bay.

Glacier Bay has few hiking trails and in the backcountry foot travel is done along riverbanks, on ridges or across ice remnants of glaciers. The only developed trails are in Bartlett Cove.

❸ Gustavus

About 9 miles from Bartlett Cove is the small settlement of Gustavus, an interesting backcountry community. The town's 400 citizens include a mix of professional people – doctors, lawyers, former government workers and artists – who decided to drop out of the rat race and live on their own in the middle of the woods. Electricity only arrived in the early 1980s and in some homes you must pump water at the sink or build a fire before you can have a hot shower.

Gustavus has no downtown: it's little more than an airstrip left over from WWII and a road to Bartlett Cove, known to most locals as 'the Road.' Along the Road there is little to see, as most cabins and homes are tucked away behind a shield of trees.

The state ferry docks at Gustavus and Alaska Airlines jets land at the small airport nearby.

CORALIE MATHIEU/SHUTTERSTOCK ©

Bartlett Cove

Left: Glacier Bay National Park from above;
Right: Brown bear

❹ Glacier Bay Lodge

This is essentially a national park lodge
(p68) and the only accommodations in the
park itself. Located at Bartlett Cove, 8 miles
northwest of Gustavus, the self-contained
lodge has 55 rooms, a crackling fire in a
huge stone fireplace and a dining room
that usually hums in the evening with an
interesting mixture of park employees,
backpackers and locals from Gustavus.

Nightly slide presentations, ranger talks
and movies held upstairs cover the park's
natural history.

Packages with bed, breakfast and an
eight-hour park boat tour go for around
$645 for two people.

Essential Information

Sleeping

Most of the accommodations are in Gustavus, which adds a 7% bed-and-sales tax. The **Glacier Bay Lodge** (📞888-229-8687; www.visitglacierbay.com; 199 Bartlett Cove Rd; r $219-249; 🕙May-Sep) is 8 miles out of town at Bartlett Cove.

Tourist Information

Glacier Bay National Park Visitor Center (📞907-697-2661; www.nps.gov/glba; 🕙11am-8pm) On the 2nd floor of Glacier Bay Lodge, this center has exhibits, a bookstore and an information desk. There are also daily guided walks from the lodge, park films and slide presentations.

Gustavus Visitors Association (📞907-697-2454; www.gustavusak.com) Has loads of information on its website.

Visitor Information Station (📞907-697-2627; 🕙7am-8pm May-Sep) Campers, kayakers and boaters can stop at the park's Visitor Information Station at the foot of the public dock in Bartlett Cove for backcountry and boating permits, logistical information and a 20-minute orientation video.

Getting There & Away

The cheapest way to reach Gustavus is via the **Alaska Marine Highway** (📞800-642-0066; www.ferryalaska.com). Several times a week the MV *LeConte* makes the round-trip run from Juneau to Gustavus (one way $48, 4½ hours) along a route that often features whale sightings. **TLC Taxi** (📞907-697-2239) meets most ferry arrivals and also charges $15 per person for a trip to Bartlett Cove.

Alaska Airlines (📞800-426-0333; www.alaskaair.com) Offers the only jet service, with a daily 25-minute trip from Juneau to Gustavus.

Alaska Seaplanes (📞907-789-3331; www.flyalaskaseaplanes.com) Has up to five flights per day between Gustavus and Juneau for $119 one way. ∎

Top left: Glacier Bay cruise; Top right: Female moose; Bottom: Alaska Marine Highway

MELISSAMN/SHUTTERSTOCK ©

Katmai National Park

A national park since 1980, Katmai is famous for its salmon-trapping brown bears, epic sport-fishing and unusual volcanic landscapes. Unconnected to the main Alaskan road network, a visit here, for most people, is a once-in-a-lifetime experience involving meticulous pre-planning and a big wad of cash.

Great For...

State
Alaska

Entrance Fee
Free

Area
6395 sq miles

Nearly all park visitors fly in via floatplane to the main tourist area of **Brooks Camp**, 35 miles east of King Salmon. Here they will stand spine-tinglingly close to formidable 1000lb brown bears pawing giant salmon out of the river (some bears even catch the fish clean in their chops). It's the most heavily visited section of the park, equipped with a rustic lodge plus a couple of short trails.

Brooks Falls

Every year, hundreds of brown bears emerge from hibernation and make their way to Brooks Falls, a small but important waterfall in Katmai National Park. Around the same time, salmon begin their journey up Brooks River to spawn in Brooks Lake upstream. At this crossroads, salmon can be seen leaping into waiting bears' jaws. Brown bear concentrations are at their highest in July, when dozens can often be spotted at or around the falls.

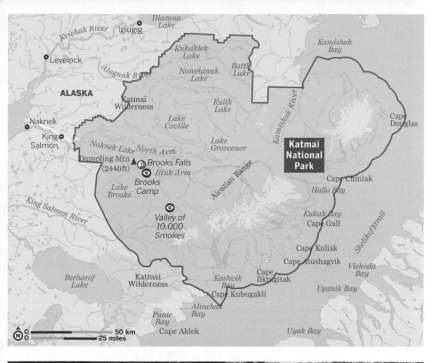

Brooks Falls

Bear Viewing

Katmai supports a healthy population of 2200 brown bears. Many of the bears arrive with instinctual punctuality at Brooks Falls on July 1 for the annual salmon spawning, which lasts until the end of the month. The bears return in September for a second showing to feed on the dead salmon carcasses.

Brooks Camp has three established bear-watching areas. From the lodge, a dirt road leads to a floating bridge over the river and the first observation deck. From here you can see the bears feeding in the mouth of the river or swimming in the bay.

Continue on the road to the Valley of Ten Thousand Smokes, and in half a mile a marked trail winds to Brooks Falls. Two more viewing platforms lie along this half-mile trail. The first sits above some shallows that occasionally draw sows trying to keep their cubs away from aggressive males at the falls.

The last deck at the falls is the prime viewing area, where you can photograph the salmon making spectacular leaps or a big brownie at the top of the cascade waiting with open jaws to catch a fish. At the peak of the salmon run, there might be eight to 12 bears here, two or three of them atop the falls themselves. The observation deck holds 40 people, and in early to mid-July it will be crammed with photographers, forcing rangers to rotate people on and off.

Brooks Camps' bear season is relatively short, but more adventurous visitors can charter floatplanes and guides to take them out to other bear-viewing areas on the coast between June and October.

Despite Katmai's dense bear population (two bears per sq mile in places) only two serious human–bear incidents have been recorded in 100 years – a testament to fine park management.

Valley of Ten Thousand Smokes

A scar in the earth left behind by the massive 1912 Novarupta volcanic eruption, the Valley of Ten Thousand Smokes is a stark landscape of deep gorges, volcanic ash and lava flows. In 1916 Robert Griggs led an expedition into the region to examine the eruption's aftermath. He found a valley of thousands of fumaroles (steam and gas vents) emitting clouds of vapor into the sky, hence the valley's name.

The post-apocalyptic spectacle served as Katmai's original raison d'être and led to the area being declared a national monument in 1918.

Visitors can access the valley by reserving a tour (from $88) through Katmailand (p74).

Hiking

Hiking and backpacking are the best ways to see the park's unusual backcountry. Like Denali National Park in Alaska's Interior, Katmai has few formal trails; backpackers follow river bars, lakeshores, gravel ridges and other natural routes. Many hiking trips begin with a ride on the park bus along the dirt road to Three Forks Overlook, in the Valley of Ten Thousand Smokes. The bus will also drop off and pick up hikers and backpackers along the road – or you can walk its full 23-mile length.

The only developed trail from Brooks Camp is a half-day trek to the top of **Dumpling Mountain** (2440ft). The trail leaves the ranger station and heads north past the campground, climbing 1.5 miles to a scenic overlook. It then continues another 2.5 miles to the mountain's summit, where there are superb views of the surrounding lakes.

Paddling

The area has some excellent paddling, including the **Savonoski Loop**, a five- to seven-day adventure. Other popular trips include a 30-mile paddle from Brooks Camp to the Bay of Islands and a 10-mile paddle to Margot Creek, which has good fishing and lots of bears.

Kayaks are the overwhelming choice for most paddlers due to high winds blowing across big lakes, and possible rough water. Accomplished paddlers should have no problem, but the conditions can sometimes get dicey for novices.

Fishing

Fishing trips are popular and rainbow trout are plentiful in the park's large lakes. In fact, most park facilities were first built to accommodate anglers. Fishing populations are carefully managed by Katmai National Park and Alaska Department of Fish and Game. Sport fishing licenses are required for nonresidents aged 16 and older and most residents 16 to 59. Further regulations exist depending on where anglers cast their reels.

Because fishers and brown bears are often attracted to the same catch, anglers must be careful when fishing in Katmai and follow safe bear country practices such as maintaining bear awareness, cutting the line if a bear approaches and safe catch storage.

CSNATZGER/SHUTTERSTOCK ©

Valley of Ten Thousand Smokes

Essential Information

Package Tours

Because of the logistics of getting there and the need to plan and reserve so much in advance, many visitors arrive in Katmai as part of a one-call-does-it-all package tour. A shockingly large number are part of a one-day visit, spending large sums of money for what is basically an hour or two of bear watching.

Getting There & Away

Most visitors to Katmai fly from Anchorage into King Salmon on Alaska Airlines (☎800-252-7522; ww.alaskaair.com) for between $450 and $600 round-trip. Once you're in King Salmon, a number of air-taxi companies offer the 20-minute floatplane flight out to Brooks Camp. **Katmai Air** (☎800-544-0551, 907-243-5448; www.katmaiair.com), the Katmailand-affiliated company, charges $228 for a round-trip.

Companies like **Regal Air** (☎907-243-8535; www.regal-air.com; 4506 Lakeshore Dr) and **Rust's Flying Service** (☎907-243-1595; www.flyrusts.com; 4525 Enstrom Circle) offer day trips straight from Anchorage, but the 2½-hour flight aboard a cramped floatplane, plus limited time with the bears, make this a less-ideal option.

Sleeping

If you plan to stay at Brooks Camp, either at the lodge or in the campground, you must make a reservation. Otherwise, you're limited to staying in King Salmon and visiting the park on day trips.

Grosvenor Lodge, Kulik Lodge and Brooks Lodge are all operated by concessionaire **Katmailand** (☎907-243-5448, 877-771-1849; www.katmailand.com). Two-night stays start at $1602 per person (double occupancy) and include round-trip flights from Anchorage.

Independent options like **Katmai Wilderness Lodge** (www.katmai-wilderness.com) provide alternatives. ∎

Top left: Brooks Camp; Top right: Fishing near Brooks Falls; Bottom: Dumpling Mountain

PATRICK CIVELLO/SHUTTERSTOCK ©

Exit Glacier

Kenai Fjords National Park

Kenai Fjords National Park was created in 1980 to protect 587,000 acres of Alaska's most awesome, impenetrable wilderness. Crowning the park is the massive Harding Ice Field; from it, countless tidewater glaciers pour down, carving the coast into dizzying fjords. Road-accessible Exit Glacier is its highlight attraction.

With such a glaciated landscape – and an abundance of marine wildlife – the park is a major tourist attraction. Unfortunately, it's also an expensive one. That is why road-accessible Exit Glacier is its highlight attraction. Hardier souls can ascend to the Harding Ice Field from the same trail-head, but only experienced mountaineers equipped with skis, ice axes and crampons can investigate the 900 sq miles of ice.

The majority of visitors either take a quick trip to Exit Glacier's face or splurge on a tour-boat cruise along the coast. For those who want to spend more time in the park, the coastal fjords are a blue-water kayaker's dream.

Exit Glacier

The marquee attraction of Kenai Fjords National Park is Exit Glacier, named by explorers crossing the Harding Ice Field who found the glacier a suitable way to 'exit' the ice and mountains.

Great For...

State
Alaska

Entrance Fee
Free

Area
917 sq miles

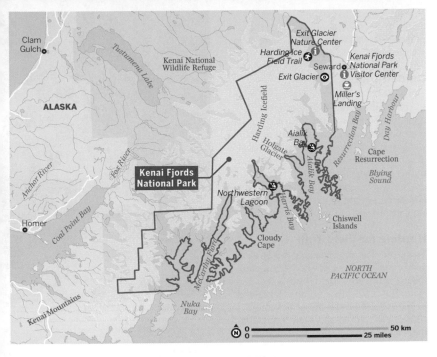

From the Exit Glacier Nature Center (p79), the **Outwash Plain Trail** is an easy three-quarter-mile walk to the glacier's alluvial plain – a flat expanse of pulverized silt and gravel, cut through by braids of gray meltwater. The **Edge of the Glacier Trail** leaves the first loop and climbs steeply to an overlook at the side of the glacier before returning. Both trails make for a short hike that will take one or two hours; you can return along the half-mile **nature trail** through cottonwood forest, alder thickets and old glacial moraines before emerging at the ranger station. Note how the land becomes more vegetated the further you get from the ice, the result of having had more time to recover from its glacial scouring. Signs indicate how far the glacier extended.

If you have the time and legs for it, the hike up to the **Harding Ice Field** (p78) is well worth it; where else can you see a large remnant of the Pleistocene Ice Age?

Paddling

Blue-water paddles out of Resurrection Bay along the coastline of the park are for experienced kayakers only; others should invest in a drop-off service. You'll be rewarded, however, with wildlife encounters and close-up views of the glaciers from a unique perspective.

With several glaciers to visit, **Aialik Bay** is a popular arm for kayakers. Many people hire water-taxis to drop them near Aialik Glacier, then take three or four days to paddle south past Pedersen Glacier and into Holgate Arm, where they're picked up. The high point of the trip is Holgate Glacier, an active tidewater glacier that's the main feature of all the boat tours.

Northwestern Lagoon is more expensive to reach but much more isolated, with not nearly as many tour boats. The wildlife is excellent, especially the seabirds and sea otters, and more than a half-dozen glaciers can be seen. Plan on three to four days if you're being dropped inside the lagoon.

Most companies can arrange drop-off and pick-up; it's about $300 for the round-trip to Aialik Bay; prices decrease or increase depending on distance.

Guided Tours

The easiest and most popular way to view the park's dramatic fjords, glaciers and abundant wildlife is from a cruise ship. Several companies offer the same basic tours: wildlife cruises (three to five hours) take in W without really entering the park. Don't bother taking the short cruise, unless you are really trying to avoid seasickness. Much better tours (eight to 10 hours) explore Holgate Arm or Northwestern Lagoon.

Harding Ice Field Trail

This strenuous and yet extremely popular 4-mile trail (six- to eight-hour round-trip) follows Exit Glacier up to Harding Ice Field. The 700-sq-mile expanse remained unknown to white settlers until the early 1900s, when a map-surveying team found that eight coastal glaciers flowed from the exact same system.

Today you can rediscover it via a steep, roughly cut and sometimes slippery ascent to 3500ft. Beware of bears; they're common here. Only experienced glacier-travelers should head onto the ice field proper.

The trek is well worth it for those with the stamina, as it provides spectacular views of not only the ice field but Exit Glacier and the valley below. The upper section of the route is snow-covered for much of the year; bring a jacket and watch for ice-bridges above creeks. Camping up here is a great idea, but the free, tiny public-use cabin at the top is for emergencies only. ∎

Top left: Hiking the Harding Ice Field Trail;
Top right: Kayaking Aialik Bay; Bottom: Harding Ice Field

Essential Information

Getting There & Away

To reach the coastal fjords, you'll need to take a tour or catch a water-taxi with **Miller's Landing** (907-331-3113; www. millerslandingak.com). Getting to Exit Glacier is a bit easier. If you don't have a car, the **Exit Glacier Shuttle** (907-224-5569; www.exitglaciershuttle.com; round-trip $15; 9:30am-5pm Mon-Thu, from 8:30am Fri-Sun) runs an hourly shuttle to the glacier. The van scoops passengers up in downtown Seward and at the small-boat harbor.

Sleeping

A few lovely options exist in the park, but for all except Exit Glacier Camp-ground you'll need a water-taxi.

Tourist Information

Exit Glacier Nature Center (9am-8pm) At the Exit Glacier trailhead; has interpretive displays, sells field guides, and is the starting point for ranger-guided hikes.

Kenai Fjords National Park Visitor Center (907-224-3175; 9am-7pm) Located in Seward's small-boat harbor; has info on hikes and paddles in the park.

TOP LEFT: MELISSAMN/SHUTTERSTOCK © TOP RIGHT: PATRICK CIVELLO/SHUTTERSTOCK © BOTTOM: ATTILIO PREGNOLATO/SHUTTERSTOCK ©

Lake Clark

Lake Clark National Park

Only 100 miles southwest of Anchorage, Lake Clark National Park features spectacular scenery that is a composite of Alaska: an awesome array of tundra-covered hills, mountains, glaciers, coastline, the largest lakes in the state and two active volcanoes.

Great For...

State
Alaska

Entrance Fee
Free

Area
6296 sq miles

The centerpiece of the park is a 45-mile shimmering body of turquoise water fringed by the snowy summits of glacier-tipped peaks. The park is also where the Alaska Range merges into the Aleutian Range to form the Chigmit Mountains, and is home to two volcanoes: Mt Iliamna and Mt Redoubt. Despite its overwhelming scenery and close proximity to Alaska's largest city, fewer than 5000 visitors a year make it to this 6296-sq-mile preserve.

Water Activities

Kayaking and canoeing are popular ways to explore the lake itself, the shores of which range from craggy horizons to low tundra. In the park's main town, Port Alsworth, **Tulchina Adventures** (www. tulchinaadventures.com) will rent kayaks (per day single/double $65/100) or set up an unguided kayak/camping trip ($475 for two people for one night).

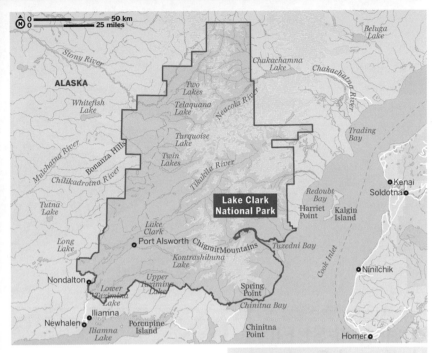

Hiking

The hiking is phenomenal, but Lake Clark is best suited to the experienced backpacker. For any pre-trip planning, visit the park website, which has the latest guidance on traveling in the backcountry.

Port Alsworth has a **visitor center** ([ℐ]907-781-2218; 1 Park Pl; ⊗8am-5pm Mon-Fri, 9am-6pm Sat & Sun) with displays and videos on the park. There you'll find information on both the **Telaquana Trail Route**, a historic Dena'ina Athabascan route running from Telaquana Lake to Kijik Village, and **Twin Lakes**, where dry tundra slopes provide easy travel to ridges and great views.

Float Trips

Float trips down any of the three designated wild rivers (the **Chilikadrotna**, **Tlikakilaand** and **Mulchatna**) are spectacular and exciting, with waterways rated from class III to class IV. The best way to

Essential Information

To reach the park, you will need to arrange with an Anchorage charter pilot for drop-off at the start of your adventure (around $490 round-trip).

organize a boat rental is through **Alaska Raft & Kayak** (www.tulchinaadventures. com), which rents out inflatable sea kayaks and canoes (per day $65) and 14ft rafts (per day $100) in Anchorage. The shop will also deliver the boat to **Lake Clark Air** ([ℐ]907-781-2208, 888-440-2281; www. lakeclarkair.com) in Anchorage for your flight into the national park and pick it up when you return. ∎

MINT IMAGES - FRANS LANTING/GETTY IMAGES ©

Wrangell-St Elias National Park

Imagine an area the size of Switzerland. Now strip away its road network, eradicate its cities and take away all but 40 of its eight million people. The result would be something approximating Wrangell-St Elias National Park, a feast of brawny ice-encrusted mountains that make up the second-largest national park in the world.

Great For...

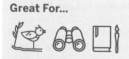

State
Alaska

Entrance Fee
Free

Area
20,625 sq miles

One more time: this park is *big*. If Wrangell-St Elias were a country it would be larger than 70 of the world's independent nations. Its biggest glacier covers an area larger than the US state of Rhode Island. Plenty of its mountain peaks have never been climbed. And that's even before you've started counting the bears, beavers, porcupines and moose.

❶ McCarthy

Alaska doesn't lack isolated frontier towns that act as magnets for a colorful cast of folk who want to live away from everything, and nor does it suffer a paucity of tourist destinations. But it's a rare place that manages to bridge the gap between these two identities – a spot that is authentically on the edge of civilization, yet welcomes those curious folk who want to peep in on the raw, wild pulse of the Alaskan bush.

Enter McCarthy. Once the red-light district and drinking strip for bored miners

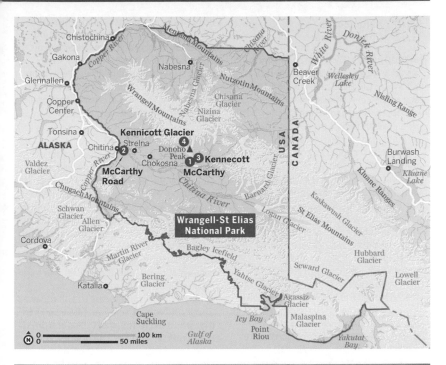

McCarthy

Kennecott's Copper Boom

In 1900 miners 'Tarantula Jack' Smith and Clarence Warner reconnoitered Kennicott Glacier's east side until they arrived at a creek and found traces of copper. They named the creek Bonanza, and was it ever – the entire mountainside turned out to hold some of the richest copper deposits ever uncovered.

Eventually, a group of investors bought the existing stakes and formed the Kennecott Copper Corporation, named when a clerical worker misspelled Kennicott (which is why, nowadays, the town is spelled with an 'e' while the river, glacier and other natural features have an 'i'). First the syndicate built its railroad: 196 miles of track through the wilderness, including the leg that's now McCarthy Rd and Cordova's famous Million Dollar Bridge. The line cost $23 million before it even reached the mines in 1911.

From 1911 until 1938 the mines operated around the clock and reported a net profit of more than $100 million. By 1938 most of the rich ore had been exhausted, and in November that year the mine was closed permanently. With the exception of a steam turbine and two large diesel engines, everything was left behind, and Kennecott became a perfectly preserved slice of US mining history.

Unfortunately, when the railroad bed was converted to a road in 1974, Kennecott also became the country's biggest help-yourself hardware store. Locals were taking windows, doors and wiring, while tourists were picking the town clean of tools, railroad spikes and anything else they could haul away as souvenirs.

In 1998 the NPS purchased the mill, power plant and many of the buildings from private owners as the first step to restoring them.

bivouacked at the 'dry' mining town of Kennecott, today this is an intersection of muddy streets and a few dozen locals and seasonal workers, who work hard, play harder, and generally live life with an unvarnished gusto that's a joy to witness. It helps that they live in a valley that could give Eden a fit of jealousy.

❷ McCarthy Road

There's only one way you can get to McCarthy by land: the bumpy, unpaved McCarthy Rd. This dirt route is a rump-shaker, but even a regular car can make it if you go slow (35mph maximum) and stay in the center to avoid running over old rail spikes – contact **Ma Johnson's Hotel** (☏907-554-5402; www.mccarthylodge.com; Main St; d/tr $229/299) in McCarthy about car-rental companies that will let you take their vehicles on the road.

Much of the route traces the abandoned Copper River and Northwest Railroad bed that was used to transport copper from the mines to Cordova. The first few miles offer spectacular views of the Chugach Mountains, the east–west range that separates the Chitina Valley lowlands from the Gulf of Alaska. Peaks average 7000ft to 8000ft. Below is the mighty Copper River, one of the world's great waterways for king and red salmon.

❸ Kennecott

Between 1911 and 1938, the mining outpost of Kennecott was the serious 'dry' working town to free-living, hard-drinking McCarthy. These days it is effectively an open-air museum on mining history, as well as the jump-off point for several excellent hikes.

Old mill town constitutes pretty much all of present-day Kennecott. Dozens of old wood and log buildings have been restored, stabilized or purposely left in a state of decrepitude. You're welcome to wander around the outside of the buildings at will, or you can join daily tours.

Concentration Mill & Leaching Plant

Like a rickety fantasy hatched out of a lunatic's dream, this 14-story **building** (tour $28) in Kennecott once processed the copper mined out of the surrounding mountains. You can only enter via two-hour tours led by **St Elias Alpine Guides** (☎907-554-4445; www.steliasguides.com), but this is highly recommended for a chance to peek into a truly surreal tableau of 20th-century mining equipment.

There are three tours daily. St Elias Alpine Guides has a small kiosk at the entrance to Kennecott, where the shuttle drops off passengers.

Root Glacier Trail

Beginning at the far edge of town past the Concentration Mill, the Root Glacier Trail is an easy 4- or 8-mile round-trip route out to the sparkling white-and-blue ice. Signposts mark the route and the path itself is clear and well used as far as the primitive Jumbo Creek campsites.

From here you can head left to the glacier or continue straight another 2 miles along a rougher track. At the end, the Erie Mine Bunkhouse will be visible on the slopes above you. Check at the visitor center for the latest on the trail conditions. Most of this trail can also be ridden on a mountain bike.

Bonanza Mine Trail

This excellent hike from Kennecott follows an alpine trail – a round-trip of almost 9 miles. Begin on the Root Glacier Trail and turn off to the right at the clearly marked junction. This is a steep uphill walk with 3800ft of elevation gain. Once above the tree line, the view of the confluence of the Root and Kennicott Glaciers is stunning.

Expect three to five hours for this hike up if the weather is good and half that time to return. Water is available at the top, but carry at least a quart if the day is hot. Snow lingers higher up until early June.

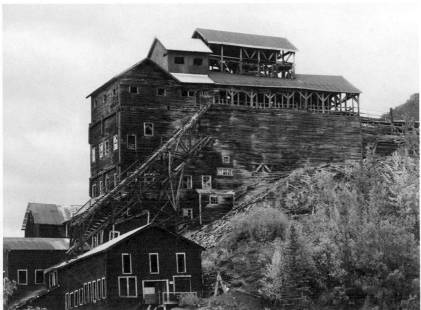

The former Kennecott Copper Mine

MICHAEL HEFFERNAN/LONELY PLANET ©

Left: Root Glacier Trail;
Right: Pool on Kennicott Glacier

❹ Kennicott Glacier

'Oh no, they destroyed this valley!' If you're like 99% of visitors, that's exactly what you'll think as you reach Kennecott and look across the valley at a rolling landscape of dirt and rubble. But no, that isn't a dump of mine tailings from the copper-boom days, but the Kennicott Glacier moraine. The ice is buried underneath.

The glacier is thinning terribly and has dropped 175ft in height over the past eight decades. To put that statistic in perspective, back in the 1930s some locals didn't even realize they lived in a valley, as the ice field was so high.

Essential Information

Be honest: had you heard about Wrangell-St Elias before you cracked open this book? If so, we nod our heads in respect. For every eight tourists who track north to Denali, only one intrepid traveler tackles the little-known wilderness of Wrangell. Why? Good question. Granted, most of the park is desolate and doesn't have the infrastructure or satellite towns of Denali, though it did have its improbable copper-mining history, preserved for posterity by the NPS.

So, how do you tackle such an immense place? Most visitors enter the park via the tiny, off-the-grid settlements of McCarthy and Kennecott, accessible by bush plane or a single unpaved road that branches off the Richardson Hwy near Copper Center. Between them, these hamlets have several eating establishments, a store and a hardy year-round population of around 40 people who hunt and grow their own vegetables. Popular activities in the area include glacier hiking, ice climbing and historical tours of Kennecott's mine buildings.

You don't need a backcountry permit for overnight hikes, but you are encouraged to leave an itinerary at any of the ranger stations, where you can also get advice and a bear-proof canister for your trip. There's a refundable deposit required for the canister.

You can also drop by the visitor center in Kennecott for maps and ideas for both day and overnight hikes. There are literally two full folders of options. Popular overnight hikes include Donoho Peak, Erie Lake and McCarthy Creek.

Sleeping

There are numerous privately owned and operated campsites, B&Bs and roadhouses all around the borders of the park, as well as lodges and hotels within areas like McCarthy and along the Nabesna Rd. Wrangell-St Elias is also home to 14 *very* basic public-use backcountry cabins. Most are first-come, first-served, but three can be reserved on the park website (www.nps.gov/wrst). No permit is required for backcountry camping; use bear-proof food containers. ∎

Lake on Kennicott Glacier

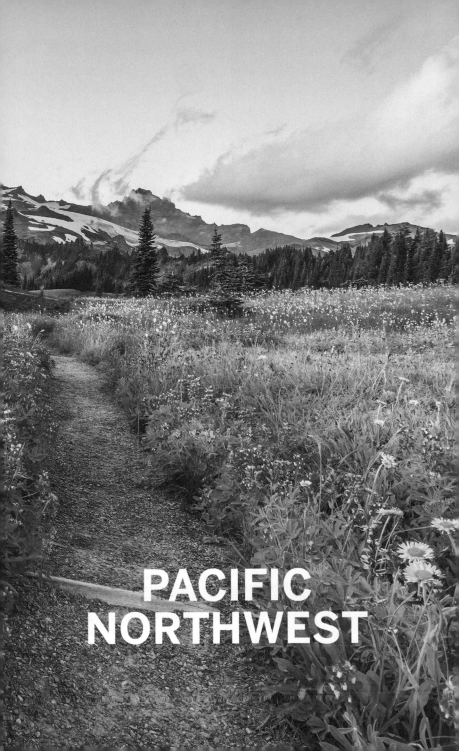

PACIFIC
NORTHWEST

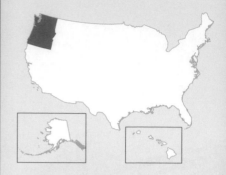

Pacific Northwest

Locked away from the rest of the country, caught between the Pacific Ocean and the Rockies, the Pacific Northwest is a unique world of lush rainforests and volcanic peaks. Glacial snowfields emerge from a sea of clouds, and virgin stands of massive Douglas fir and red cedar serve as reminders of what the continent's ancient forests must have once looked like. Throughout the Pacific Northwest, everything seems greener, until Mt Rainier and Crater Lake steal the limelight as glorious, snow-bound mountain realms.

Don't Miss

○ Seeing the moss-draped trees of the thick, wet Hoh Rain Forest in Olympic (p122)

○ Hiking among wildflower meadows by Mt Rainier (p104)

○ Taking in the North Cascades scenery of glaciers and jagged peaks (p116)

○ Exploring the beauty of America's deepest lake at Crater Lake (p94)

○ Soaking in scenic hot springs and enjoying the rush of Toketee Falls in Crater Lake (p102)

When to Go

All of the parks enjoy a short but intense high season between early June and early September with sunny, warm days and good chances of seeing wildflowers and big fauna. High season also means crowds, competition for reservations, and higher prices for accommodations.

In shoulder season (April, May and October), crowds, prices and some services drop off. Although temperatures remain mild, rain is always possible.

While parks technically remain open year-round, you'll need to be a hardy soul to enjoy them in the winter. Then again, for ski resorts, the busiest times are December to March.

Previous page: Mt Rainier (p104)

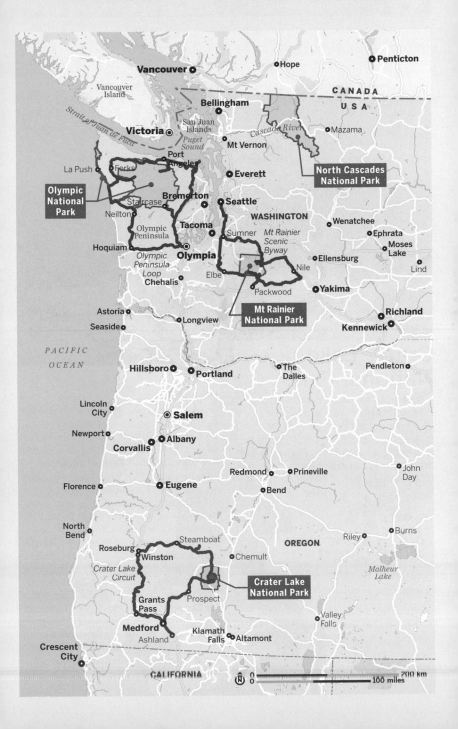

H PETER JI PHOTOGRAPHER/SHUTTERSTOCK ©

Crater Lake National Park

The gloriously blue waters of Crater Lake reflect surrounding mountain peaks like a giant dark-blue mirror, making for spectacular photographs and breathtaking panoramas. Crater Lake is Oregon's only national park and also the USA's deepest lake at 1943ft deep.

Great For...

State
Oregon

Entrance Fee
7-day pass per vehicle/pedestrian $25/12

Area
287 sq miles

Hiking

Crater Lake has over 90 miles of hiking trails, though some higher ones aren't completely clear of snow until late July. From the eastern edge of the Rim Village parking lot, a 1.7-mile trail leads up 8054ft **Garfield Peak** to an expansive view of the lake; in July the slopes are covered with wildflowers. A strenuous 5-mile round-trip hike takes you to an even better lake vista atop 8929ft **Mt Scott**, the highest point in the park. For a steep but shorter hike, trek up 0.7 miles to the **Watchman**, an old lookout tower on the opposite side of the lake that boasts one of the park's best views. For flower enthusiasts, there's an easy 1-mile nature trail near the **Steel Visitor Center** (☎541-594-3000; ⊘9am-5pm May-Oct, 10am-4pm Nov-Apr) that winds through the **Castle Crest Wildflower Garden Trail**.

The popular and steep mile-long **Cleetwood Cove Trail**, at the northern end of the crater, provides the only water access at the

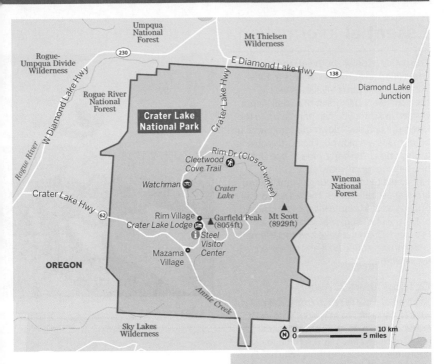

cove. Two-hour **boat tours** (📞888-774-2728; www.craterlakelodges.com/activities/volcano-boat-cruises; Cleetwood Cove boat dock; adult/child $42/28; ⏱late Jun–early Sep) are available; reserve, as these are popular.

Skiing & Snowshoeing

In winter, only the southern entrance road to Rim Village is kept plowed to provide access to several Nordic skiing trails. Rentals are unavailable inside the park, so bring skis with you. Only experienced skiers should attempt the dangerous, avalanche-prone loop around Crater Lake, which takes two to three days and requires a backcountry permit from park headquarters.

Snowshoes are provided for free ranger-led snowshoe walks, which are held at 1pm on weekends from Thanksgiving through March or April; call 📞541-594-3100 for reservations.

Mt Mazama

The ancient mountain whose remains now form Crater Lake was Mt Mazama, a roughly 12,000ft volcanic peak that was heavily glaciered and inactive for many thousands of years until it came back to life 7700 years ago. A catastrophic explosion scattered ash for hundreds of miles as flows of superheated pumice solidified into massive banks. These eruptions emptied the magma chambers at the heart of the volcano, and the summit cone collapsed to form the caldera.

Only snowfall and rain contribute to the lake water. This purity and the lake's great depth give it that famous blue color. Sparse forests can be seen growing in pumice and ash in the Pumice Desert, just north of Crater Lake along N Entrance Rd.

Essential Information

The park's popular south entrance is open year-round and provides access to Rim Village and Mazama Village, as well as the park headquarters at the Steel Visitor Center. In winter you can only go up to the lake's rim and back down the same way; no other roads are plowed. The north entrance is only open from early June to late October, depending on snowfall.

It's best to top up your gas tank before arriving at Crater Lake. There's reasonably priced gas at Mazama Village (summertime only); the closest pumps otherwise are in Prospect, Diamond Lake and Fort Klamath.

Summer is often cold and windy, so dress warmly.

Getting There & Away

You'll need a car to reach Crater Lake; it's wise to carry chains in winter. The north entrance and most of the roads inside the park are closed from November usually until June. Hwy 62 and the 4-mile road from the highway to park headquarters are plowed and open year-round. The 3-mile road from headquarters to Rim Village is kept open when possible, but heavy snowfall means it may be closed; call ahead to check (☏541-594-3100).

Sleeping

Other than **Crater Lake Lodge** (☏888-774-2728; www.craterlakelodges.com; r from $220; ⏱late May–mid-Oct; 📶) which is the only lodging at the lake, and Mazama Village (7 miles from the rim), the nearest noncamping accommodations are 20 to 40 miles away. Park lodging is closed mid-October to late May, depending on snowfall. Fort Klamath has several good lodgings. Union Creek, Prospect, Diamond Lake and Lemolo Lake all have nice, woodsy places to stay, and there's lots of accommodations in Medford, Roseburg and Klamath Falls.

Top left: Hikers on Garfield Peak (p94); Top right: Castle Crest Wildflower Garden Trail (p94); Bottom: Crater Lake

CLASSIC ROAD TRIPS

Crater Lake Circuit

Make it a (big) day trip or stay a week – serene, mystical Crater Lake is one of Oregon's most enticing destinations. The best route takes you on a heavily forested, waterfall-studded loop.

Duration 2–3 days

Distance 365 miles

Best Time to Go
Late May to mid-October when all the roads are open.

Essential Photo
No surprise here: Crater Lake.

Best Waterfall
Two-tiered Toketee Falls is our favorite.

❶ Ashland

A favorite base for day trips to Crater Lake, Ashland is bursting at the seams with lovely places to sleep and eat (though you'll want to book your hotel room far in advance during the busy summer months). Home of the **Oregon Shakespeare Festival** (OSF; ☑541-482-4331; www.osfashland.org; cnr Main & Pioneer Sts; tickets $30-136; ⏱Tue-Sun Feb-Oct), it has more culture than most towns its size, and is just far enough off the highway to resist becoming a chain-motel mecca.

It's not just Shakespeare that makes Ashland the cultural heart of southern Oregon. If you like contemporary art, check out the **Schneider Museum of Art** (☑541-552-6245; http://sma.sou.edu; 1250 Siskiyou Blvd; suggested donation $5; ⏱10am-4pm Mon-Sat).

Ashland's historic downtown and lovely **Lithia Park** (59 Winburn Way) make it a dandy place to go for a walk before or after your journey to Crater Lake.

The Drive » Medford is 13 miles north of Ashland on I-5.

❷ Medford

Southern Oregon's largest metropolis is where you hop off I-5 for your trek out to Crater Lake, and it can also serve as a suitable base of operations if you want a cheap, convenient place to bunk down for the night.

On your way out, check out the **Table Rocks**, impressive 800ft mesas that speak of the area's volcanic past and are home to unique plant and animal species. Flowery spring is the best time for hiking to the flat tops, which were revered Native American sites. After **TouVelle State Park** (Table Rock Rd), fork either left to reach the trailhead to Lower Table Rock (3.5-mile round-trip hike) or right for Upper Table Rock (2.5-mile round-trip hike).

The Drive » The drive along Hwy 62 isn't much until after Shady Cove, when urban sprawl stops and forest begins. Your next stop is 45 miles northeast in Prospect.

❸ Prospect

No wonder they changed the name of Mill Creek Falls Scenic Area – that implies you're just going to see another waterfall (not that there's anything wrong with that). But the real treat at **Prospect State Scenic Viewpoint** is hiking down to the **Avenue of Giant Boulders**, where the Rogue River crashes dramatically through huge chunks of rock and a little bit of scrambling offers the most rewarding views.

Take the trail from the southernmost of two parking lots on Mill Creek Dr. Keep left to get to the boulders or right for a short hike to two viewpoints for **Mill Creek Falls** and **Barr Creek Falls**. If you've got one more falls-sighting left in you, take the short hike from the upper parking lot to the lovely **Pearsony Falls**.

Lithia Park

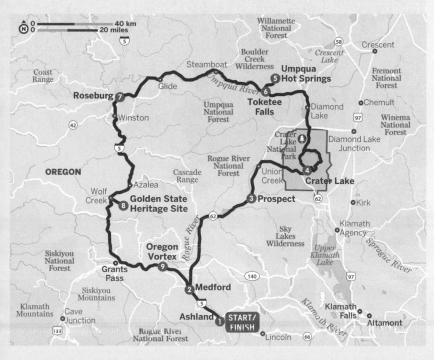

The Drive » Follow Hwy 62 for another 28 miles to get to the Crater Lake National Park turnoff at Munson Valley Rd.

❹ Crater Lake

This is it: the main highlight and reason for being of this entire trip is Oregon's most beautiful body of water, **Crater Lake** (☎541-594-3000; www.nps.gov/crla; 7-day vehicle pass $25). This amazingly blue lake is filled with some of the clearest, purest water you can imagine – you can easily peer 100ft down – and sits inside a 6-mile-wide caldera created when Mt Mazama erupted nearly 8000 years ago. Protruding from the water and adding to the drama of the landscape is **Wizard Island**, a volcanic cinder cone topped by its own mini crater called Witches Cauldron.

Get the overview with the 33-mile **Rim Drive** (⊙Jun–mid-Oct), which offers over 30 viewpoints as it winds around the edge of Crater Lake. The gloriously still waters reflect surrounding mountain peaks like a giant dark-blue mirror, making for spectacular photographs and breathtaking panoramas.

You can also camp, ski or hike in the surrounding old-growth forests. The popular and steep mile-long **Cleetwood Cove Trail**, at the north end of the crater, provides the only water access at the cove. Or get up close with a two-hour boat tour (p95).

The Drive » Head north on Hwy 138 for 41 miles and turn right on Rd 34.

❺ Umpqua Hot Springs

Set on a mountainside overlooking the North Umpqua River, Umpqua Hot Springs is one of Oregon's most splendid hot springs, with a little bit of height-induced adrenaline thanks to its position atop a rocky bluff.

Top: Table Rocks; Bottom left: Umpqua Hot Springs; Bottom right: Mill Creek Falls

SHERRI R. CAMP/SHUTTERSTOCK ©

LEFT: JOSHUA RAINEY/ALAMY STOCK PHOTO ©; RIGHT: CHARLES WOLLERTZ/ALAMY STOCK PHOTO ©

Springs are known for soothing weary muscles, so earn your soak at Umpqua by starting with a hike – it is in a national forest, after all – where you'll be treated to lush, old-growth forest and waterfalls punctuating the landscape. Half a mile from the parking lot is the scenic **North Umpqua Trail**.

The Drive » The turnout for Toketee Falls is right on Hwy 138, 2 miles past the Umpqua turnoff.

❻ Toketee Falls

More than half a dozen waterfalls line this section of the Rogue-Umpqua Scenic Byway, but the one that truly demands a stop is the stunning, two-tiered **Toketee Falls** (USFS Rd 34). The falls' first tier drops 40ft into an upper pool behind a cliff of columnar basalt, then crashes another 80ft down the rock columns into yet another gorgeous, green-blue pool below. One tiny disclaimer: although the hike is just 0.4 miles, there's a staircase of 200 steps down to the viewpoint, so climbing back up to your car is a bit of a workout.

The Drive » From here, the scenery tapers back down to only moderately spectacular as you leave the Umpqua National Forest. It's just one hour to Roseburg.

❼ Roseburg

Sprawling Roseburg lies in a valley near the confluence of the South and North Umpqua Rivers. The city is mostly a cheap, modern sleepover for travelers headed elsewhere (such as Crater Lake), but it does have a cute, historic downtown area and is surrounded by award-winning wineries.

Don't miss the excellent **Douglas County Museum** (📞541-957-7007; www.umpquavalleymuseums.org; 123 Museum Dr, I-5 exit 123; adult/child $8/2; ⏲10am-5pm Tue-Sat), which displays the area's cultural and natural histories. Especially interesting are the railroad derailment photos and History of Wine exhibit. Kids have an interactive area and live snakes to look at.

The Drive » Go south on I-5 for 47 miles and take the Wolf Creek exit. Follow Old State Hwy 99 to curve back under the interstate. Golden is 3.2 miles east on Coyote Creek Rd.

❽ Golden State Heritage Site

Not ready to return to civilization quite yet? Stop off in the ghost town of **Golden**, population zero. A former mining town that had over 100 residents in the mid-1800s, Golden was built on the banks of Coyote Creek when gold was discovered there.

A handful of structures remain, as well as some newfangled interpretive signs that tell the tale of a curiously devout community that eschewed drinking and dancing, all giving a fascinating glimpse of what life was like back then. The weathered wooden buildings include a residence, the general store/post office, and a classic country church. Fun fact: the town was once used as a location for the long-running American Western TV series *Gunsmoke*.

The Drive » Go south another 45 miles on I-5 and take exit 43. The Oregon Vortex is 4.2 miles north of the access road.

❾ Oregon Vortex

Just outside the town of Gold Hill lies the **Oregon Vortex** (📞541-855-1543; www.oregonvortex.com; 4303 Sardine Creek L Fork Rd, Gold Hill; adult/child $12.75/9; ⏲9am-4pm Mar-Oct, to 5pm Jun-Aug), where the laws of physics don't seem to apply – or is it all just an optical illusion created by skewed buildings on steep hillsides? However you see it, the place is definitely bizarre: objects roll uphill, a person's height changes depending on where they stand, and brooms stand up on their own...or so it seems. ∎

Toketee Falls

Mt Rainier National Park

Emblazoned on every Washington license plate and visible throughout much of the western state, Mt Rainier is the contiguous USA's fifth-highest peak and, in the eyes of many, its most awe-inspiring.

Great For...

State
Washington

Entrance Fee
7-day pass per vehicle/pedestrian $30/15

Area
368 sq miles

The mountain's snowcapped summit and forest-covered foothills boast numerous hiking trails, swaths of flower-carpeted meadows and an alluring peak that presents a formidable challenge for aspiring climbers. The park website includes downloadable maps and descriptions of 50 park trails.

❶ Paradise

Aside from hiding numerous trailheads and being the starting point for most summit hikes, Paradise guards the iconic Paradise Inn (built in 1916) and the large, informative **Henry M Jackson Visitor Center** (☏360-569-6571; ⊙10am-5pm daily May-Oct, Sat & Sun Nov-Apr), which holds a cutting-edge museum with hands-on exhibits on everything from flora to glacier formation and shows a must-see 21-minute film entitled *Mount Rainier: Restless Giant*.

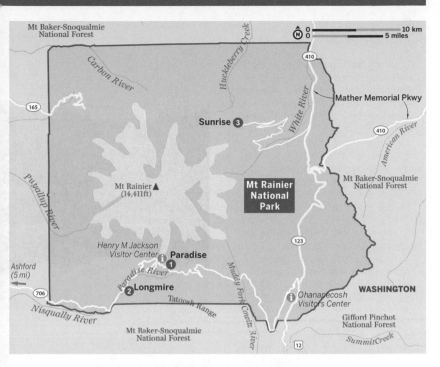

Park naturalists lead free interpretive hikes from the visitor center daily in summer, and snowshoe walks on winter weekends.

The daughter of park pioneer James Longmire unintentionally named this high mountain nirvana, when she exclaimed what a paradise it was on visiting this spot for the first time in the 1880s. Suddenly, the high-mountain nirvana had a name, and a very apt one at that. One of the snowiest places on earth, 5400ft-high Paradise remains the park's most popular draw, with its famous flower meadows backed by dramatic Rainier views on the days (a clear minority annually) when the mountain decides to take off its cloudy hat.

The Paradise area is crisscrossed with trails, of all types and standards, some good for a short stroll (with the kids), others the realm of more serious hikers. For a medium-pacer, hike the 5-mile **Skyline Trail**, starting behind the Paradise Inn and climbing approximately 1600ft to Panorama Point, with good views of Mt Rainier and the neighboring Tatoosh Range.

❷ Longmire

The **National Park Inn** (✆360-569-2275; Hwy 706; r with shared/private bath from $132/187; ❄) – built in classic 'parkitecture' style – has stood here since 1917. It's complemented by park offices, the tiny, free **Longmire Museum** (✆360-569-6575; Hwy 706; ⊙9am-4:30pm May-Jul) and a number of important trailheads. James Longmire first came here in 1883 and noticed the hot mineral springs that bubbled up in a lovely meadow opposite the present-day National Park Inn. The next year he established Longmire's Medicinal Springs, and in 1890 he built the Longmire Springs Hotel.

❸ Sunrise

Mt Rainier's main eastern entrance is the gateway to Sunrise, which at 6100ft

Climbing Mt Rainier

Close to Puget Sound's urban areas and unobstructed by other peaks, Mt Rainier has an overwhelming presence, set off by its 26 glaciers, and it has long enraptured the millions of inhabitants who live in its shadow. Though it's an iconic peak to bag, climbing Rainier is no picnic; old hands liken it to running a marathon in thin air with crampons stuck to your shoes. Approximately 9000 people attempt it annually, but only half of them make it to the top.

Hazard Stevens and PB Van Trump made the first documented Mt Rainier summit in 1870.

The most popular route starts at Paradise and involves a brief night's rest at Camp Muir before you rise between midnight and 2am to don crampons and ropes for the climb over Disappointment Cleaver and the Ingraham Glacier to the summit. All climbers going higher than Camp Muir must register at the **Paradise Ranger Station** next to the Henry M Jackson Visitor Center (p104). Excellent four-day guided ascents are led by **Rainier Mountaineering Inc** (📞888-892-5462; www.rmiguides.com; 30027 Hwy 706 E, Ashford; 4-day climb $1163).

marks the park's highest road. Thanks to the superior elevation here, the summer season is particularly short and snow can linger well into July. The area is also noticeably drier than Paradise, resulting in an interesting variety of subalpine vegetation, including masses of wildflowers.

The views from Sunrise are famously spectacular and – aside from stunning close-ups of Mt Rainier itself – you can also, quite literally, watch the weather roll in over the distant peaks of Mts Baker and Adams. Similarly impressive is the glistening Emmons Glacier, which, at 4 sq miles in size, is the largest glacier in the contiguous USA.

Top left: Mount Rainier; Top right: Old lodge in Mt
Rainier National Park; Bottom: Fall in the park

Essential Information

Getting There & Away
For the most part, you're better off
driving yourself, but there are also tour
options out of Seattle.

Nisqually Entrance
This southwestern corner of Mt Rainier
National Park is its most developed
(and hence most visited) corner. Here
you'll find the only year-round road and
the gateway settlements of Ashford
and Copper Creek, which offer plenty
of useful park-related facilities.

Hwy 706 enters the park about 1½
hours' drive southeast of Seattle. After
the entry tollbooth, a well-paved road
continues east, offering the first good
views of Mt Rainier – weather permit-
ting. At the 7-mile mark you'll pass
Longmire (p105). From here the road
climbs steeply for 12 miles, passing
numerous hairpin turns and viewpoints
until it emerges at the elevated alpine
meadows of Paradise (p104).

Sleeping
There are camping and lodge options
in the park and plenty of other types
of lodging outside, mostly along the
Longmire entrance route.

TOP LEFT: NADIA YONG/SHUTTERSTOCK © TOP RIGHT: OKSANA PERKINS/SHUTTERSTOCK © BOTTOM: MARK A LEE/SHUTTERSTOCK ©

CLASSIC ROAD TRIPS

Mt Rainier Scenic Byways

Wrapped in a 368-sq-mile national park, and standing 2000ft higher than anything else in the Pacific Northwest, Rainier is a mountain of biblical proportions.

Duration 2–3 days

Distance 454 miles

Best Time to Go
June to October when alpine flowers bloom.

Essential Photo
Rainier's snow-topped summit reflected in Reflection Lakes.

Best Alpine Meadows
A toss-up between Paradise and Sunrise.

❶ Seattle

Seattle is an appropriate place to start this epic circuit around what locals refer to reverently as 'the Mountain.' Before heading off, take some time to walk around, seeking out the soul of the city at **Pike Place Market** (www.pikeplacemarket.org; 85 Pike St; ⏰9am-6pm Mon-Sat, to 5pm Sun; 🚇Westlake) 🚩 – for that's where it hides. On the rare days when Rainier reveals itself from the cloudy heavens, you can also wander down to the waterfront for a glimpse of the high-altitude glories to come.

The Drive » There is little to delay you out of Seattle until the tiny town of Elbe,

72 miles away. Drive south on I-5 to exit 154A, then east on I-405, and south again on SR-167 and SR-161. Just southwest of Eatonville, SR-161 merges with SR-7; follow this road into Elbe on the cusp of the national park.

❷ Elbe

The pinprick settlement of Elbe (population 29) has two claims to fame: its tiny white Lutheran **church** built by German immigrants in 1906 (and positively ancient by Pacific Northwest standards), and the heritage **Mt Rainier Scenic Railroad** (www.mtrainierrailroad.com). Due to the COVID-19 pandemic, the railroad has ceased operations for the foreseeable future. But aping the railway theme is the **Hobo Inn & Diner** (www.rrdiner.com; 54106 Mountain Hwy E; r from $115), whose restaurant, bar and rooms all inhabit vintage, lovingly tended, cabooses (train carriages).

The Drive » From Elbe take SR-706 (the National Park Hwy) due east to Ashford.

❸ Ashford

Situated a couple of miles outside the busy Nisqually entrance, Ashford is the national park's main service center with some medium-ranking accommodations, an info center and **Whittaker's Motel & Bunkhouse** (📞360-569-2439; www.whittakersbunkhouse.com; 30205 SR 706 E; dm $40, d $90-145; 📶), a hostel-cafe conceived by legendary local mountaineer Lou Whittaker in the early 1990s. It would be heresy to leave town without popping inside for an espresso before grabbing brunch (or lunch) down the road at the **Copper Creek Inn** (📞360-569-2326; www.coppercreekinn.com; 35707 SR 706 E; breakfast from $8, burgers $10, dinner mains $12-29; ⏰11am-8pm Mon-Fri, 8am-9pm Sat, 8am-8pm Sun, opens earlier in summer), where the wild blackberry pies have fueled many a successful summit attempt.

The Drive » Just east of Ashford on SR-706 you'll see the park entrance gate.

❹ Nisqually Entrance

The southwestern Nisqually entrance (named for the nearby river, which in turn is named after a local Native American tribe) is the busiest in **Mt Rainier National Park** and the only year-round entry gate. The simple entrance arch was built in 1922. Pay your park fee at the ticket window. As you drive through the entrance, you'll notice how, almost immediately, the trees appear denser and older. Many of these moss-covered behemoths date back over 700 years and measure up to 200ft in height.

The Drive » Follow the road alongside the Nisqually River for a couple of miles to Kautz Creek, where the summit of Rainier appears like a ghostly apparition.

❺ Longmire

Worth a stop to stretch your legs or gain an early glimpse of Rainier's mossy old-growth forest, Longmire was the brainchild of a certain James Longmire who first

came here in 1883 during a climbing trip when he noticed the hot mineral springs that bubbled up in a lovely meadow opposite the present-day National Park Inn (p105). He and his family returned the following year and established Longmire's Medicinal Springs, and in 1890 he built the Longmire Springs Hotel. Since 1917 the National Park Inn has stood on this site and is complemented by a small store, the tiny Longmire Information Center & Museum (p105) and a number of important trailheads. For a laid-back look at some old-growth forest and pastoral meadows, try the **Trail of the Shadows Loop**, a 0.8-mile circuit that begins across the road from the museum.

The Drive » After Longmire the road slowly starts to climb, passing the Cougar Rock Campground and Christine Falls, both on the left. A couple of miles after the falls, bear right onto a short stretch of summer-only one-way road (signposted 'Viewpoint') for a view stop at Ricksecker Point.

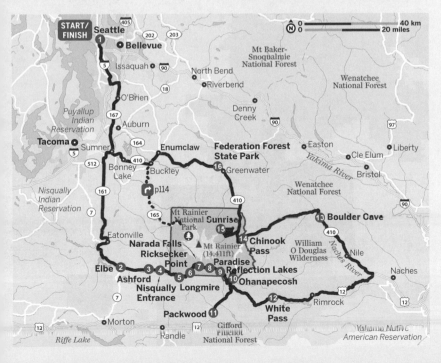

⑥ Ricksecker Point

One of the park's premier viewpoints beloved by photographers, professional or otherwise, Ricksecker Point is a fine place to study five of Rainier's 26 glaciers – Nisqually, Pyramid, Success, Kautz and Wilson. The summit you see here is actually a false one (Point Success); the obscured *true* summit is 257ft higher. Equally majestic to the southeast is the saw-toothed Tatoosh Range.

The Drive » Rejoin the main road and continue uphill.

⑦ Narada Falls

Eight miles east of Longmire, a parking area marks the starting point for a steep 0.2-mile trail that leads down through flowers and ferns to the misty 168ft Narada Falls. The falls, often embellished by brilliant rainbows, carry the Paradise River over a basalt cliff. In high season, expect to get a face-full of water spray and an earful of oohing and ahhing as this is the park's most popular waterfall. In winter the falls freeze over and attract daring ice-climbers.

The Drive » Soon after the falls, the road forks; stay left for Paradise. Follow the winding asphalt for another 2 miles to the Upper Parking Lot.

⑧ Paradise

In the elevated alpine meadows of Paradise (p104) you'll find the area's biggest and best information center–museum, the Henry M Jackson Visitor Center (p104), which was completely rebuilt and reopened in 2008.

It's also home of the iconic **Paradise Inn** (☏ 360-569-2275; r with shared/private bath from $123/182; ☺May-Oct; ☏), which was built in 1916 and also refurbished in

GERARDO MARTINEZ CONS/GETTY IMAGES ©

Top: Pike Place Market, Seattle; Bottom left: View from Ricksecker Point; Bottom right: Narada Falls

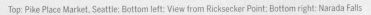

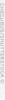

☀ Summer Wonderland

You've circumnavigated it in a car; now how about walking it? Rainier is not only encircled by a road; you can also walk around it on foot via the long-distance Wonderland Trail. Laid out in 1915, the 93-mile-long precipitous path initially served as a patrol beat for park rangers and in the 1930s it was briefly earmarked as a paved ring road for cars. Fortunately, the plan never reached fruition and today the unbroken trail (which gains 21,000ft in cumulative elevation) is one of the most challenging and iconic hikes in the Pacific Northwest. You'll need food, camping gear, eight to 12 free days and a permit from the Longmire Information Center & Museum (p105) to do Wonderland. Longmire is a popular start point. There are 18 backcountry campgrounds en route; reservations ($20) are advisable in peak season (July and August). The official park page (www.nps.gov/mora) has more information.

2008. Designed to blend in with the environment and constructed almost entirely of local materials, including the exposed cedar logs in the Great Room, the inn was an early blueprint for National Park–rustic architecture. Following the two-year, $30-million, earthquake-withstanding revamp, the smallish rooms retain their close-to-the-wilderness essence, while the communal areas are nothing short of regal.

The Drive » Drive out of the east end of the Paradise Upper Parking Lot, cross the Paradise River (looking out for marmots) and descend the one-way road for 2 miles to a junction. Turn left and rejoin the main two-way road heading toward Reflection Lakes and Steven's Canyon.

❾ Reflection Lake

Rainier eyes itself in the mirror on calm cloudless days at Reflection Lake, formed during a violent volcanic eruption nearly 6000 years ago. You can pull over for double-vision photos of the mountain framed by tufts of precious wildflowers. The main lake used to have a boat concession, but now it's deliciously tranquil bar the odd passing tour bus.

The Drive » Avalanche chutes plague the U-shaped Steven's Canyon Rd in the winter, ensuring it remains closed outside peak season (unlike Paradise on the western side). Seen from above, the canyon is rather spectacular. Stop for a bird's-eye view a mile or so after Reflection Lakes before the trees close in. From here it's downhill all the way to Ohanapecosh.

❿ Ohanapecosh

Ohanapecosh (o-*ha*-nuh-peh-*kosh*) – the name means 'at the edge' – in the park's southeastern corner is usually accessed by the small settlement of Packwood, 12 miles to the southwest on US 12, which harbors a small number of eating and sleeping options. Shoehorned between Mt Rainier and its two southern neighbors, Mt St Helens and Mt Adams, this is a good base for travelers wanting to visit two or more of the mountains.

Just inside the Steven's Canyon gate, you'll find the 1.5-mile **Grove of the Patriarchs Trail**, one of the park's most popular short hikes. The trail explores a small island in the Ohanapecosh River replete with craning Douglas fir, cedar and hemlock trees, some of which are over 1000 years old. To reach the **Ohanapecosh Visitor Center** (⏰9am-5pm May–mid-Oct), turn right at the Steven's Canyon entrance onto SR-123 and drive 1.5 miles south. Alternatively, you can hike down from the Grove of the Patriarchs.

The Drive » Go right at the Steven's Canyon entrance and follow SR-123 south past the visitor center to the intersection with US 12. For Packwood, bear right.

⓫ Packwood

A service center for Mt St Helens, Mt Rainier and the nearby ski area of White Pass, Packwood is what in the Old West they called a 'one-horse town.' A few low- to mid-ranking eating joints and accommodations glued to US 12 provide a good excuse to pull over and mingle with other road-trippers. Chin-waggers congregate at **Mountain Goat Coffee** (📞360-494-5600; https://facebook.com/MountainGoatCoffeeCo/; 105 E Main St; pastries from $2; ⊗7am-5pm), where you may run into a park ranger or two.

The Drive » Retrace your route to the intersection of US 12 and SR-123. The climb to White Pass begins here. Stop at a pullover soon after the intersection to appreciate the indelible sight of Mt Rainier as it appears briefly above the trees.

⑫ White Pass

Higher than Snoqualmie and Stevens Passes to the north, White Pass carries a quieter, open-year-round road that, at various points, offers glimpses of three Cascadian volcanoes: Mt Rainier, Mt Adams and Mt St Helens. The pass itself, perched at 4500ft, is home to an understated **ski area** (www.skiwhitepass.com; day passes adult/ child $62/43), which has one condo complex for overnighters. Otherwise, people stay in nearby Packwood or drive up for the day from Yakima.

The Drive » A classic east–west Washington scenery shift kicks in soon after White Pass as you follow US 12 amid

Grove of the Patriarchs Trail

Detour:
Carbon River Entrance

Start: **16** Federation Forest State Park

The park's northwest entrance is its most isolated and undeveloped corner, with two unpaved (and unconnected) roads and little in the way of facilities, save a lone ranger station and the very basic **Ipsut Creek Campground** (360-829-5127). But while the tourist traffic might be thin on the ground, the landscape lacks nothing in magnificence.

Named for its coal deposits, Carbon River is the park's wettest region and protects one of the few remaining examples of inland temperate rain forest in the contiguous USA. Dense, green and cloaked in moss, this verdant wilderness can be penetrated by a handful of interpretive trails that fan off the Carbon River Rd.

Getting here takes you part of the way back to Seattle. Take Hwy 410 W to 116 S (Carbon River Rd) then turn left. After about 15.5 miles you'll come to the Carbon River ranger station just before the entrance.

increasingly scattered trees and bald, steep-sided river coulees. At the intersection with SR-410, swing north on the Chinook Scenic Byway just west of the town of Naches to reach Boulder Cave, 65 miles from White Pass.

13 Boulder Cave

Among the many excuses to pull over on this stretch of the Chinook Scenic Byway is **Boulder Cave** (May-Oct), a rarity in the relatively cave-free terrain of the Pacific Northwest and doubly unique due to its formation through a combination of volcanic and erosive processes. A 2-mile round-trip trail built by the Civilian Conservation Corp in 1935 leads into the cave's murky interior, formed when Devil's Creek cut a tunnel through soft sedimentary rock, leaving hard volcanic basalt on top. Up to 50 rare big-eared bats hibernate in

the cave each winter, when it is closed to the public. Bring a flashlight.

The Drive » Continue west and uphill toward Chinook Pass, 25 miles from Boulder Cave, as the air cools and the snowdrifts pile up roadside.

14 Chinook Pass

Closed until May and infested with lingering snowdrifts well into July, Chinook Pass towers 5430ft on Rainier's eastern flank. The long-distance **Pacific Crest Trail** crosses the highway here on a pretty stone bridge, while nearby **Crystal Mountain** (360-663-2265; www.crystalmountainresort.com; 33914 Crystal Mountain Blvd, Hwy 410) comprises Washington's largest ski area and only bona fide overnight 'resort.' Rather than stop at the pass, cruise a few hundred yards further west to **Tipsoo Lake**, another reflective photographer's dream where a paved trail will return the blood to your legs.

The Drive » From Tipsoo Lake the road winds down to relatively 'low' Cayuse Pass (4694ft). Turn north here and descend a further 1000ft in 3 miles to the turning for Mt Rainier's White River entrance. This is the gateway to Sunrise, 16 miles uphill via a series of switchbacks.

15 Sunrise

The highest point you can drive to within the park, Sunrise (p105) is known for its spectacular views. If you want to go for a walk, a trailhead directly across the parking lot from the **Sunrise Lodge Cafeteria** (snacks $6-9; 10am-7pm Jul & Aug) provides access to **Emmons Vista**, with good views of Mt Rainier, Little Tahoma and the Emmons Glacier. Nearby, the 1-mile **Sourdough Ridge Trail** leads to pristine subalpine meadows for stunning views over other volcanic giants.

The **Sunrise Visitors Center** (10am-6pm daily, early Jul-early Sep) is a helpful spot, where you can check out the exhibits or take part in an interpretive hike.

The Drive » Coast downhill to the White River entrance and turn north onto the

Mather Memorial Pkwy in order to exit the park. In the small community of Greenwater on SR-410 you can load up with gas and food.

⑯ Federation Forest State Park

Just when you thought you'd left ancient nature behind, up springs Federation Forest State Park, created by a foresighted women's group in the 1940s in order to preserve a rapidly diminishing stock of local old-growth forest from logging interests. Today its fir, spruce, hemlock and cedar trees cluster around the lackadaisical White River, while the **Catherine Montgomery Interpretive Center** (⊙8am-dusk) offers a rundown of the contrasting ecosystems of east–west Washington state. There's also a bookstore and 12 miles of trails, most of them family friendly. ∎

Sourdough Ridge Trail

ROMAN KHOMLYAK/SHUTTERSTOCK ©

OKSANA PERKINS/SHUTTERSTOCK ©

North Cascades National Park

Inaugurated in 1968, North Cascades National Park is Alaska transplanted into the lower 48, half a million acres of dramatic, daunting wild country strafed with mountains, lakes, glaciers (over 300 of them) and wildlife, but with almost no trace of civilization.

Erratic weather, massive precipitation, thick rainforest and vertiginous cliffs have long ensured the remoteness of the park's mountains: steep, alpine behemoths furnished with names like Mt Terror, Mt Fury, Mt Despair and Forbidden Peak. Aspiring bushwhackers and free-climbers love the unique challenges offered by this eerie wilderness. The less adrenaline-hungry stick close to arterial Hwy 20 and prepare for the drive of a lifetime.

Hiking

It's possible to get a basic overview of this vast alpine wilderness by motoring through in a car on US 20, making use of the numerous pullouts and short interpretive hikes that are scattered along the route. But in order to taste the park's real gritty essence you'll need a tent, a decent rucksack and a gung-ho sense of adventure.

Great For...

State
Washington

Entrance Fee
Free

Area
789 sq miles

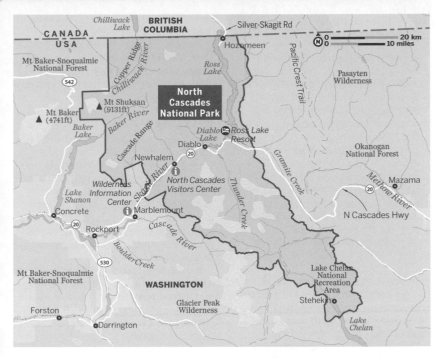

Cascade Pass Trail

Three-piece Park

For administrative reasons, the park is split into two sections – north and south – separated in the middle by the Ross Lake National Recreation Area, which encases a spectacular 20-mile section of the North Cascades Hwy (US 20). Along the park's southern border around Stehekin lies a third region, the Lake Chelan National Recreation Area, a 62,000-acre protected park that surrounds the fjord-like Lake Chelan. To avoid confusion, the three zones are managed as one contiguous area and overlaid by the Stephen Mather Wilderness, created in 1988.

Free permits are required for backcountry camping in the park and must be obtained in person from the Wilderness Information Center (p120) or at a park ranger station.

One of the park's most challenging but rewarding day hikes is the strenuous **Sourdough Mountain Trail**, which gains a mile in height for the 5.5 miles (one way) traveled on the ground. Most say that the effort is worth it; the views of Cascadian peaks and turquoise Diablo Lake 5000-plus feet below are some of the best in the park.

The 3.7-mile hike to 5384ft **Cascade Pass** is the best loved in these mountains, and gets you very quickly up into a flower-carpeted, glacier-surrounded paradise that will leave you struggling for superlatives.

From the southern end of the Colonial Creek Campground (Mile 130, Hwy 20), the long **Thunder Creek Trail** leads along a powerful glacier-fed river through old-growth forest and clumps of wildflowers flourishing in the dank forest. After 2.5 miles the **Fourth of July Trail** branches left to a pass of the same name and makes a good early-season hike (10 miles round-trip from the campground). Alternatively, you

can continue along Thunder Creek to Park Creek Pass and, ultimately, Stehekin.

Just past the Ross Dam trailhead at Mile 134.5, the easy and wheelchair-accessible **Happy Creek Forest Walk** (0.5 miles) gives you an up-close look at the forest on a raised boardwalk.

Ross Lake

Ross Lake (Hwy 20, Mile 134) stretches north for 23 miles, across the Canadian border, but – in keeping with the wild terrain – is accessible only by trail or water. Incorporated into the Ross Lake National Recreation Area, the lake was formed by the building of the Ross Dam, an ambitious hydroelectric project, from 1937, designed to generate electricity for the fast-growing Seattle area.

You can hike down to the Ross Dam from a trailhead on Hwy 20. The trail descends for 1 mile and crosses over the dam. For an extra leg-stretch you can follow the west bank of Ross Lake another mile to Ross Lake Resort (p120).

Rafting

Although it doesn't offer the heart-in-the-mouth white-water runs of less tamed waterways, the dam-controlled Upper Skagit makes for a good class II or III family trip through old-growth forest, offering plenty of opportunities for wildlife-watching. A number of companies offer excursions here, including **Alpine Adventures** (www.alpineadventures.com; day trips per person from $79).

Diablo Lake

Just below Ross Lake, **Diablo Lake** (supply ferries adult/child one way $10/5) is held back by the similarly huge 389ft **Diablo Dam**. A pullout off Hwy 20 known as the **Diablo Dam Overlook** provides incredible views of the turquoise-green lake framed by glacier-capped peaks.

Diablo was the world's highest arch-type dam at the time of its completion in 1930, and building it in such a hostile region with no road access was one of the greatest engineering feats of the interwar period.

Diablo Lake is popular with kayakers and canoeists (there's a launch site at Colonial Creek Campground). The water's turquoise hue is a result of powdered rock ground down by glaciers.

North Cascades Environmental Learning Center (www.ncascades.org) 🍃, on the lake's northern banks, is operated by the North Cascades Institute in partnership with the National Park Service.

Diablo Dam

Essential Information

Getting There & Away

You'll need your own wheels to get into and around the national park.

Taking the Supply Boat

If you're heading to the **Ross Lake Resort** (☏206-386-4437; www.rosslakeresort.com; 503 Diablo St, Rockport; cabins $205-385; ⊙mid-Jun–late Oct) you can access it by hiking or taking one of the twice-daily boat and supply truck combos (round-trip $20). The resort has a car park and ferry dock situated on the right just after you cross the Diablo Dam. The first boat leaves at 8:30am and turns around at the Ross Powerhouse dock at 9am. The second leaves Diablo at 3pm and turns around at 3:30pm. Visitors can take the ferry one way and hike back to the Diablo Dam on the moderate 3.8-mile Diablo Lake Trail.

Tourist Information

North Cascades Visitors Center (☏206-386-4495, ext 11; 502 Newhalem St, Newhalem; ⊙9am-5pm daily Jun-Sep, Sat & Sun May & Oct) ✔ A walk-through exhibit mixes informative placards about the park's ecosystems with nature videos. Expert rangers will enlighten you on everything from melting glaciers to the fickleness of the weather. Various short trails track the Skagit River and Newhalem Creek, the longest of which is the 1.8-mile River Loop Trail. Rangers give interpretive talks in the vicinity in summer.

Wilderness Information Center (7280 Ranger Station Rd, Marblemount; ⊙8am-5pm early May-Jun & Sep, 7am-6pm Jul-early Sep, closed Oct-early May) Pick up backcountry permits here. ∎

Diablo Lake

SEAN PAVONE/SHUTTERSTOCK ©

Hall of Moss Trail

Olympic National Park

Olympic NP shelters a rainforest, copious glaciated mountain peaks and a 57-mile strip of coast. One of North America's great wilderness areas, most of it remains relatively untouched by humans, with 1000-year-old cedar trees juxtaposed by pristine alpine meadows, clear glacial lakes and a roadless interior.

Great For...

State
Washington

Entrance Fee
7-day pass per vehicle/pedestrian
$30/15

Area
1406 sq miles

❶ Hoh Rain Forest

The most famous section of the Olympic rain forest, the Hoh River area offers lots of hikes and an interpretive center. If you can only make one stop on the western side, this should be it. The paved Upper Hoh Rd winds 19 miles from US 101 to the visitor center, passing a **giant Sitka spruce tree** along the way. This lord of the forest is 270ft high and over 500 years old.

At the end of Hoh River Rd, the **Hoh Rain Forest Visitor Center** (📞360-374-6925; ⏰9am-4:30pm Sep-Jun, to 6pm Jul & Aug) offers displays on the ecology of the rain forest and the plants and animals that inhabit it, as well as a bookstore. Rangers lead free guided walks twice a day during summer.

Leading from the visitor center are several excellent day hikes into virgin rain forest, the most popular of which is the 0.8-mile **Hall of Moss Trail**. The 1.25-mile **Spruce Nature Trail**, another short interpretative loop, also starts at the visitor

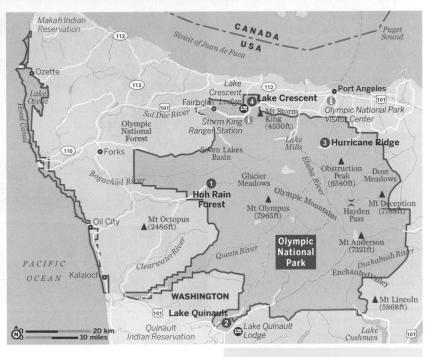

center. There is also a short wheelchair-accessible nature trail through a rain-forest marsh.

The **Hoh River Trail** is the major entry trail into the Hoh River Valley and the principal access route to Mt Olympus.

❷ Lake Quinault

The enchanting Quinault River Valley is one of the park's least crowded corners. Clustered around the lake's deep-blue waters lie forested peaks, a historic lodge and some of the oldest Sitka spruce, Douglas fir and western red cedar trees in the world. The lake itself offers plenty of activities such as fishing, boating and swimming, while upstream both the north and south branches of the Quinault River harbor a couple of important trans-park trails.

A number of short hiking trails begin just below **Lake Quinault Lodge**; pick up a free map from the US Forest Service (USFS) office. The shortest of these is the **Quinault**

Essential Information

You'll need your own car here.

You can choose to stay in one of the handful of historic park lodges, in campgrounds or in backcountry campgrounds.

The **Olympic National Park Visitor Center** (☏360-565-3100; www.nps.gov/olym; 3002 Mt Angeles Rd; ☒8am-6pm Jul & Aug, to 4pm Sep-Jun) is about a mile south of Port Angeles and is the park's most comprehensive information center. Aside from giving out excellent free maps and leaflets, the center offers children's exhibits, a bookstore, a replica of a prehistoric Makah seal-hunting canoe and a 25-minute film. Pick up a (free) detailed park map along with an even more detailed 'Wilderness Trip Planner' with backcountry trails and campgrounds marked.

Rain Forest Nature Trail, a half-mile walk through 500-year-old Douglas firs. This short trail adjoins the 3-mile **Quinault Loop Trail**, which meanders through the rain forest before circling back to the lake. The Quinault region is renowned for its huge trees. Close to the village is a 191ft Sitka spruce (purported to be up to 1000 years old), and nearby are the world's largest red cedar, Douglas fir and mountain hemlock trees.

Beyond the lake, both N Shore Rd and S Shore Rd continue up the Quinault River Valley before merging at a bridge just past Bunch Falls. From here, more adventurous hikers can sally forth into the backcountry. The area's sparkling highlight is the **Enchanted Valley Trail**.

❸ Hurricane Ridge

Hurricane Ridge is a good base for skiing, and it's the trailhead for short summer hikes to viewpoints. Hurricane Hill Trail, beginning at the end of the road leading up, and the Meadow Loop Trails, starting

Top: Lake Quinault Lodge;
Bottom: Quinault Rain Forest Nature Trail

at the **visitor center** (⊙9:30am-5pm daily summer, Fri-Sun winter), are moderately easy hikes. The first half-mile of these trails is wheelchair accessible. Note that the ridge is renowned for its fickle weather.

From Hurricane Ridge, you can drive a rough, white-knuckle 8-mile road to Obstruction Peak, laid out by the Civilian Conservation Corps (CCC) in the 1930s. Here, hikers looking for long-distance treks can pick up either the Grand Ridge Trail, which leads 7.5 miles to Deer Park, much of the way above the timberline, or the Wolf Creek Trail, an 8-mile downhill jaunt to Whiskey Bend, where it picks up the Elwha Trail.

❹ Lake Crescent

If you're heading anticlockwise on the Olympic loop from Port Angeles toward Forks, one of the first scenic surprises is luminous Lake Crescent, a popular boating and fishing area and a departure point for a number of short national park hikes.

The area is also the site of **Lake Crescent Lodge** (☑888-896-3818; www. olympicnationalparks.com; 416 Lake Crescent Rd; lodge r from $139, cabins from $309; ⊙May-Dec, limited availability winter; ❄️📶), the oldest of the park's trio of celebrated lodges – it first opened in 1916.

The best stop-off point is in a parking lot to the right of US 101 near the **Storm King Ranger Station** (☑360-928-3380; 343 Barnes Point Rd; ⊙May-Sep). A number of short hikes leave from here, including the Marymere Falls Trail, a 2-mile round-trip to a 90ft cascade that drops over a basalt cliff. For a more energetic hike, climb the side of Mt Storm King, the peak that rises to the east of Lake Crescent. The steep, 1.7-mile ascent splits off the Barnes Creek Trail.

Trout fishing is good here – the lake is deep with steep shorelines – though only artificial lures are allowed. Rowboat rentals ($15/40 per hour/half day) are available at Lake Crescent Lodge in the summer months.

Hiking Olympic National Park

There is so much beautiful wilderness to see in the park – and the best way to see it is on foot. Many visitors keep to the park's well-trodden edges on easily accessible 'touch the wilderness' hikes. Far fewer plunge into the Olympic's mossy, foggy, roadless interior.

Hikers should always take stock of weather conditions, rules and regulations, and necessary equipment. Stop in at the visitor center (p123).

Seattle Press Expedition Hike

One of the most popular cross-park treks follows the pioneering route taken by James H Christie. A former Arctic explorer, he answered the call of the *Seattle Press* newspaper in 1889 to 'acquire fame by unveiling the mystery which wraps the land encircled by the snow-capped Olympic range.' Starting at the Whiskey Bend trailhead on the Elwha River, the route tracks south and then southwest through the Elwha and Quinault River valleys to Lake Quinault, covering 44 moderately strenuous miles. It commonly takes walkers five days to complete.

Pacific Coastal Hike (North)

There are two long-distance beach hikes along the isolated coast. The more northerly is the 32.7-mile stretch between the Makah Shi Shi trailhead near Cape Flattery and Rialto Beach near La Push, which commonly makes up a moderate five-day, four-night trek. This hike stays close to the shoreline, meaning that a good understanding of tidal charts is imperative. There are 14 campgrounds en route, eight of which take reservations.

If you are contemplating a trek along the coast, request information from the National Park Service (www.nps.gov/olym), buy good maps, learn how to read tide tables and be prepared for bad weather year-round.

Top left: Hurricane Ridge; Top right: Lake Crescent Lodge; Bottom: Lake Crescent

CLASSIC ROAD TRIPS

Olympic Peninsula Loop

Freakishly wet, fantastically green and chillingly remote, the Olympic Peninsula looks like it has been resurrected from a wilder, pre-civilized era.

Duration 4 days

Distance 435 miles

Best Time to Go
June to September when deluges are slightly less likely.

Essential Photo
Hoh Rain Forest to see greens you've never imagined.

Best Wildlife
Roosevelt elk at the Hoh Rain Forest.

❶ Olympia

Welcome to Olympia, city of weird contrasts, where streetside buskers belt out acoustic grunge, and stiff bureaucrats answer their ringtones on the lawns of the expansive state legislature. A quick circuit of the **Washington State Capitol** (📞360-902-8880; 416 Sid Snyder Ave SW; ⏱7am-5:30pm Mon-Fri, 11am-4pm Sat & Sun) FREE, a huge Grecian temple of a building, will give you a last taste of civilization before you depart. Then load up the car and head swiftly for the exits.

The Drive » Your basic route is due west, initially on Hwy 101, then (briefly) on SR-8 before joining US-12 in Elma. In Grays Harbor, enter the twin cities of Aberdeen and Hoquiam, famous for producing William

Boeing and the grunge group Nirvana. Here, you swing north on Hwy 101 (again!) to leafier climes at Lake Quinault, 88 miles from Olympia.

❷ Lake Quinault

Situated in the extreme southwest of the **Olympic National Park**, the thickly forested Quinault River Valley is one of the park's least-crowded corners. Clustered on the south shore of deep-blue glacial Lake Quinault is the tiny village of **Quinault**, complete with the luscious **Lake Quinault Lodge** (📞360-288-2900; www.olympicnational parks.com; 345 S Shore Rd; r $219-450; ❋🛜🏊), a USFS office and a couple of stores.

A number of short **hiking trails** begin just below Lake Quinault Lodge; pick up a free map from the USFS office. The shortest of these is the **Quinault Rain Forest Nature Trail**, a half-mile walk through 500-year-old Douglas firs. This brief trail adjoins the 3-mile Quinault Loop Trail, which meanders through the rain forests before circling back to the lake. The Quinault region is renowned for its huge trees. Close to the village is a 191ft Sitka spruce (supposedly over 1000 years old), and nearby are the world's largest red cedar, Douglas fir and mountain hemlock trees.

The Drive » West from Lake Quinault, Hwy 101 continues through the Quinault Indian Reservation before entering a thin strip of national park territory that protects the beaches around Kalaloch (*klay*-lock). This is some of the wildest coastal scenery in the US accessible by road; various pullovers allow beach forays. After a total of 40 miles you'll reach Ruby Beach.

❸ Ruby Beach

Inhabiting a thin coastal strip that was added to the national park in 1953, Ruby Beach is accessed via a short 0.2-mile path that leads down to a large expanse of windswept coast embellished by polished black stones and wantonly strewn tree trunks. To the south toward Kalaloch, other accessible beaches include unimaginatively named Beach One through to Beach Six, all of which are popular with beachcombers.

Lake Quinault

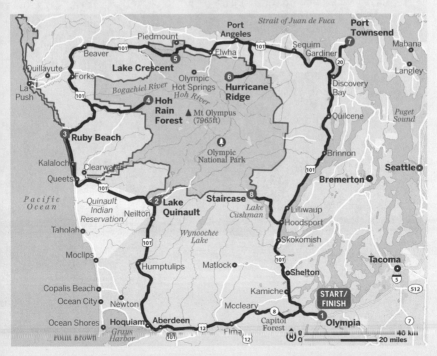

At low tide, rangers give talks on tidal-pool life at **Beach Four** and on the ecosystems of the Olympic coastal strip.

The Drive » North of Ruby Beach, Hwy 101 swings sharply northeast and inland, tracking the Hoh River. Turn right off 101 onto the Hoh River Rd to explore one of the national park's most popular inner sanctums, the Hoh Rain Forest. Suspend your excitement as the trees eerily close in as you (re)enter the park.

❹ Hoh Rain Forest

Count yourself lucky if you arrive on a day when it isn't raining! The most popular detour off Hwy 101 is the 19-mile paved road to the Hoh Valley, the densest, wettest, greenest and most intensely surreal temperate rain forest on earth. The essential hike here is the short but fascinating

Hall of Moss Trail, an easy 0.8-mile loop through the kind of weird, ethereal scenery that even JRR Tolkien couldn't have invented. Old-man's beard drips from branches above you like corduroy fringe, while trailside licorice ferns and lettuce lichens overwhelm the massive fallen trunks of maple and Sitka spruce. Rangers lead interesting free guided walks here twice a day during summer and can help you spot some of the park's 5000-strong herd of **Roosevelt elk**.

The Drive » Rejoining Hwy 101, motor north to the small and relatively nondescript but handy settlement of Forks. Press on through as Hwy 101 bends north then east through a large logging area before plunging back into the national park on the shores of wondrous Lake Crescent, which is 66 miles from the Hoh Rain Forest.

Top: Ruby Beach; Bottom left: Hall of Moss Trail; Bottom right: Roosevelt elk

The Twilight Zone

It would have been impossible to envisage 15 years ago: diminutive Forks, a depressed lumber town full of hard-nosed loggers, reborn as a pilgrimage site for 'tweenage' girls following in the ghostly footsteps of two fictional sweethearts named Bella and Edward. The reason for this weird metamorphosis was, of course, the *Twilight* saga, a four-part book series by US author Stephenie Meyer about love and vampires on the foggy Olympic Peninsula that in just a few years has shifted more than 100 million books and spawned five Hollywood movies. With Forks acting as the book's main setting, the town was catapulted to international stardom, and the cachet has yet to wear off. Daily **Twilight Tours** (360-374-5634; 130 S Spartan Ave, Forks; www.forkswa.com) visit most of the places mentioned in Meyer's books.

5 Lake Crescent

Before you've even had time to erase the horror of teenage vampires from your head, the scenery shifts again as the road winds along the glittering pine-scented shores of glacial-carved Lake Crescent. The lake looks best from water level, on a rental kayak, or from high above at its eastern edge on the **Storm King Mountain Trail** (named after the peak's wrathful spirit), accessible via a steep, 1.7-mile ascent that splits off the Barnes Creek Trail. For the less athletic, the **Marymere Falls Trail** is a 2-mile round-trip to a 90ft cascade that drops down over a basalt cliff. Both hikes leave from a parking lot to the right of SR 101 near the Storm King Ranger Station (p125). The area is also the site of the Lake Crescent Lodge (p125), the oldest of the park's trio of celebrated lodges, which first opened in 1916.

The Drive » From Lake Crescent take Hwy 101 22 miles east to the town of Port Angeles, a gateway to Victoria, Canada,

which is reachable by ferry to the north. Starting in Race St, the 18-mile Hurricane Ridge Rd climbs up 5300ft toward extensive wildflower meadows and expansive mountain vistas often visible above the clouds.

6 Hurricane Ridge

Up above the clouds, stormy Hurricane Ridge lives up to its name with fickle weather and biting winds made slightly more bearable by the park's best high-altitude views. Its proximity to Port Angeles is another bonus; if you're heading up here be sure to call into the museum-like Olympic National Park Visitor Center (p123) first. The smaller Hurricane Ridge Visitor Center (p125) has a snack bar, gift shop, toilets and is the starting point of various hikes. **Hurricane Hill Trail** (which begins at the end of the road) and the **Meadow Loop Trails** network are popular and moderately easy. The first half-mile of these trails is wheelchair accessible.

The Drive » Wind back down the Hurricane Ridge Rd, kiss the suburbs of Port Angeles and press east through the retirement community of Sequim (pronounced 'squwim'). Turn north on SR-20 to reach another, more attractive port, that of Port Townsend.

7 Port Townsend

Leaving the park momentarily behind, ease back into civilization with the cultured Victorian comforts of Port Townsend, whose period charm dates from the railroad boom of the 1890s, when the town was earmarked to become the 'New York of the West.' That never happened, but you can pick up a historic walking tour map from the **visitor center** (360-385-2722; www.ptchamber.org; 2409 Jefferson St; 9am-5pm Mon-Fri) and wander the waterfront's collection of shops, galleries and antique malls. Don't miss the old-time **Belmont Saloon** (925 Water St; mains lunch $10-14, dinner $15-32; 10:30am-2am Mon-Fri, 9am-2am Sat & Sun), the **Rose Theatre** (235 Taylor St), a gorgeously renovated theater that's been showing movies since 1908, and the fine Victorian mansions on the bluff above town, where several charming residences have been turned into B&Bs.

The Drive » From Port Townsend, head back to the junction of Hwy 101, but this time head south passing Quilcene, Brinnon, with its great diner, and the Dosewallips park entrance. You get more unbroken water views here on the park's eastern side courtesy of the Hood Canal. Track the watery beauty to Hoodsport where signs point west off Hwy 101 to Staircase, 67 miles from Port Townsend.

❽ Staircase

It's drier on the park's eastern side and the mountains are closer. The Staircase park nexus, accessible via Hoodsport, has a ranger station, campground and a decent trail system that follows the drainage of the North Fork Skokomish River and is flanked by some of the most rugged peaks in the Olympics. Nearby **Lake Cushman** has a campground and water-sports opportunities. ∎

Lake Cushman

SNE ART AND MORE/SHUTTERSTOCK ©

ROCKY MOUNTAINS

Rocky Mountains

The Rockies continue to embody the spirit of the American frontier, and the range's parks remain among the country's most prized. Yellowstone, the world's first national park, is the superstar, with primordial geysers and mega wildlife sightings at every turn. Grand Teton, Glacier and Rocky Mountain reward those in search of top-of-the-world vistas and alpine adventure, while far to the south of Colorado is the region's most curious sight – the mirage-like Great Sand Dunes.

Don't Miss

○ Spotting bears, bison and geysers at Yellowstone (p178)

○ Climbing the craggy wild trails of Grand Teton (p152)

○ Roaming the Great Sand Dunes desertscapes (p164)

○ Driving the spectacularly scenic Going-to-the-Sun Road (p149)

○ Scaling Longs Peak or just ogling its glaciated slopes from below (p172)

When to Go

With the bulk of the Rockies located at altitude with significant winter snow-cover, most visitors arrive in the summer. Full park facilities are usually open from Memorial Day (late May) to Labor Day (early September). This is when most trails are accessible, but also when the parks are busiest.

September and October bring fall foliage, some terrific lodging deals and far fewer crowds.

Many services close in the winter, although the parks remain open to avid skiers.

Previous page: Grand Teton mountains (152)

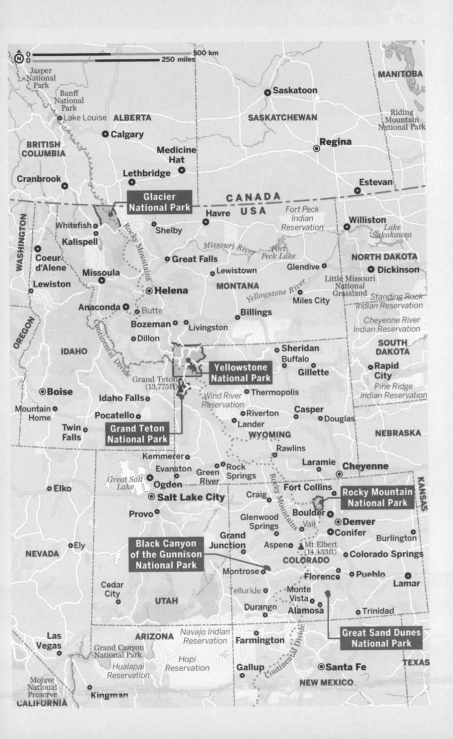

PATRICK LENIN/GETTY IMAGES ©

Black Canyon of the Gunnison National Park

The Black Canyon is the inverse geographic feature of the Rockies – a yawning chasm etched out over millions of years by the Gunnison River and volcanic uplift. Here a dark, narrow gash above the Gunnison leads down a 2000ft chasm as eerie as it is spectacular.

No other canyon in America combines the narrow openings, sheer walls and dizzying depths of the Black Canyon, and a peek over the edge evokes a sense of awe (or vertigo). In just 48 canyon miles, the Gunnison River loses more elevation than the entire 1500-mile Mississippi. This fast-moving water, carrying rock and debris, is powerfully erosive.

Great For...

State
Colorado

Entrance Fee
7-day pass per vehicle/pedestrian $20/10

Area
48 sq miles

Hiking

Short rim trails branch out from the **South Rim Visitor Center**, which has maps and information on additional hiking trails. See rangers here for a backcountry permit if you want to descend one of the South Rim's three demanding unmarked routes to the infrequently visited riverside campsites.

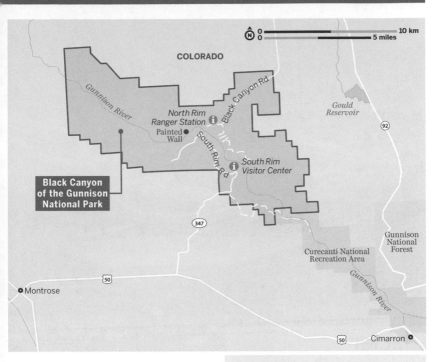

Fishing

A Colorado fishing license is required and bait fishing is not allowed – only lures and flies. If caught, all rainbow trout must be released, and a limit of four brown trout per person per day (with a bag limit of eight) applies. Fishing within 200 yards of the Crystal Dam is prohibited.

A free backcountry permit must be obtained from the South Rim Visitor Center or the North Rim Ranger Station.

South Rim Road

This 6-mile road visits 11 overlooks at the edge of the canyon, some reached via short trails up to 1.5 miles long (round-trip). At the narrowest part of Black Canyon, Chasm View is 1100ft across yet 1800ft deep. Rock climbers are frequently seen on the opposing North Wall. Colorado's highest cliff face is the 2300ft Painted Wall. ■

Essential Information

The **South Rim Visitor Center** (970-249-1915, 800-873-0244; www.nps.gov/blca; South Rim Dr; 8am-6pm late May–early Sep, 8:30am-4pm late Sep–early May) is located 2 miles past the park entrance on South Rim Dr. The more remote **North Rim Ranger Station** (North Rim; 8:30am-4pm, closed mid-Nov–mid-Apr) is accessed via Hwy 92 from Delta.

Access the park with a private vehicle. The park is 12 miles east of the US 550 junction with US 50. Exit at Hwy 347 and head north for 7 miles.

Glacier National Park

Few places on earth are as magnificent and pristine as Glacier. Protected in 1910 during the first flowering of the American conservationist movement, Glacier ranks with Yellowstone, Yosemite and the Grand Canyon among the United States' most astounding natural wonders.

Great For...

State
Montana

Entrance Fee
7-day pass per vehicle $35

Area
1489 sq miles

The glacially carved remnants of an ancient thrust fault have left a brilliant landscape of towering snowcapped pinnacles laced with plunging waterfalls and glassy turquoise lakes. The mountains are surrounded by dense forests, which host a virtually intact pre-Columbian ecosystem. Grizzly bears still roam in abundance and smart park management has kept the place accessible and authentically wild.

Glacier is renowned for its historic 'parkitecture' lodges, the spectacular Going-to-the-Sun Rd and 740 miles of hiking trails. These all put visitors within easy reach of the wild and astonishing landscapes found at the crown of the continent.

❶ Logan Pass

Perched above the tree line, atop the wind-lashed Continental Divide, and blocked by snow for most of the year, 6646ft (2026m) Logan Pass – named for William R Logan,

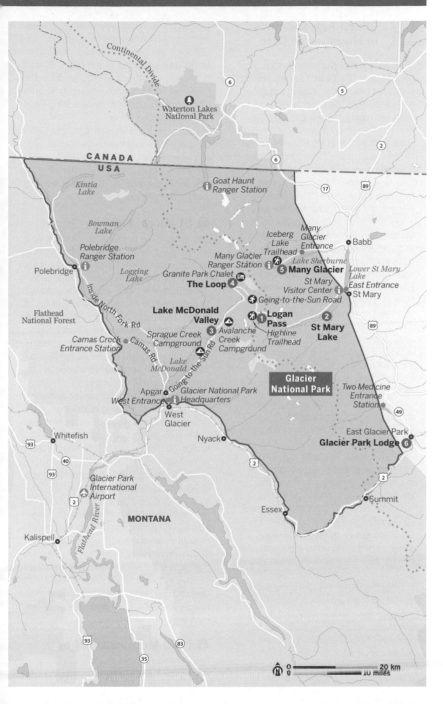

Gilded-Age Railroads to Modern Age Cars

Visitors began coming regularly to the park around 1912, when James J Hill of the Great Northern Railroad instigated an intense building program to promote his newly inaugurated line. Railway employees built grand hotels and a network of tent camps and mountain chalets, each a day's horseback ride from the next. Visitors would come for several weeks at a time, touring by horse or foot, and staying in these elegant but rustic accommodations.

But the halcyon days of trains and horse travel weren't to last. In response to the growing popularity of motorized transportation, federal funds were appropriated in 1921 to connect the east and west sides of Glacier National Park by a new road. Over a decade in the making, the legendary Going-to-the-Sun Road was finally opened in 1932, crossing the Continental Divide at 6646ft Logan Pass and opening up the park to millions.

That same year, thanks to efforts by Rotary clubs in Alberta and Montana, Glacier joined with Waterton Lakes in the world's first International Peace Park, a symbol of friendship between the USA and Canada.

WWII forced the closure of almost all hotel services in the park, and many of Glacier's rustic chalets fell into disrepair and had to be demolished. Fortunately, nine of the original 13 'parkitecture' structures survived and – complemented by two wood-paneled motor inns that were added in the 1940s – they form the basis of the park's accommodations today.

Over the years, the Going-to-the-Sun Road has been the primary travel artery in the national park and, for many, its scenic highlight. Still sporting its original stone guardrail and embellished with myriad tunnels, bridges and arches, the road has been designated a National Historic Landmark.

Glacier's first superintendent – is the park's highest navigable point by road. Two trails, Hidden Lake Overlook (which continues on to **Hidden Lake** itself) and Highline, lead out from here. Views are stupendous; the parking situation, however, is not – you might spend a lot of time searching for a spot during peak hours.

Certainly in the most magnificent setting of all the park's visitor centers, the building at **Logan Pass** (☑406-888-7800; Going-to-the-Sun Rd; ⊙9am-7pm Jun-Aug, 9:30am-4pm Sep) has park information, interactive exhibits and a good gift shop.

❷ St Mary Lake

Located on the park's drier eastern side, where the mountains melt imperceptibly into the Great Plains, St Mary Lake lies in a deep, glacier-carved valley famous for its astounding views and ferocious winds. Overlooked by the tall, chiseled peaks of the Rockies and still dramatically scarred by the landscape-altering effects of the 2006 Red Eagle Fire, the valley is spectacularly traversed by the Going-to-the-Sun Road and punctuated by numerous trailheads and viewpoints.

St Mary's gorgeous turquoise sheen, easily the most striking color of any of Glacier's major bodies of water, is due to the suspension of tiny particles of glacial rock in the lake's water that absorb and reflect light.

The **St Mary Visitor Center** (east end of Going-to-the-Sun Rd; ⊙8am-6pm mid-Jun–mid-Aug, 8am-5pm early Jun & Sep) houses interesting exhibits on wildlife, geology and Native American culture and history, as well as an auditorium featuring slide shows and ranger talks. For over 35 years, the Native America Speaksprogram has connected visitors with the stories, history and culture of the Blackfeet, Salish and Kootenai tribes. Check the seasonal schedule for days and times.

❸ Lake McDonald Valley

Greener and wetter than the St Mary Valley, the Lake McDonald Valley harbors the park's largest lake and some of its densest and oldest temperate rainforest. Crisscrossed by a number of popular trails, including the wheelchair-accessible, 0.8-mile Trail of the Cedars, the area is popular with drive-in campers, who frequent the Sprague Creek and Avalanche Creek campgrounds, as well as winter cross-country skiers who use McDonald Creek and the Going-to-the-Sun Road as seasonal skiing trails.

❹ The Loop

This sharp hairpin bend acts as a popular trailhead for hikers descending from the Granite Park Chalet and the Highline Trail. Consequently, it's normally chock-a-block with cars. The slopes nearby were badly scarred by the 2003 Trapper Fire, but nature and small shrubs are beginning to reappear.

❺ Many Glacier

Anchored by the historic 1915 Many Glacier Lodge and sprinkled with more lakes than glaciers, this picturesque valley on the park's east side has some tremendous

Red Bus Tours

Glacier's stylish red 'Jammer' buses (so-called because drivers had to 'jam' hard on the gears) are iconic park symbols. Guided tours take visitors along a dozen routes, from 3-hour trips to 8-hour journeys.

The open-roof buses were introduced on the Going-to-the-Sun Road between 1936 and 1939. They have thus been serving the park loyally for nearly 80 years, save for a two-year sabbatical in 1999 when the fleet was reconfigured by the Ford Motor Company. After an extensive makeover, they are safer, sturdier and 93% more environmentally friendly (now running off propane gas). In 2015, the company introduced a bus outfitted to serve passengers with disabilities.

The drivers provide excellent information about what you are seeing during the drive, though the four-person seats can be cramped and you may not have the best views from the middle.

COLE STECYK/SHUTTERSTOCK ©

Hidden Lake

hikes, some of which link to the Going-to-the-Sun Rd. A favorite is the 9.4-mile (return) **Iceberg Lake Trail**, a steep but rewarding jaunt through flower meadows and pine forest to an iceberg-infested lake.

❻ Glacier Park Lodge

Set in attractive, perfectly manicured flower-filled grounds overlooking Montana's oldest golf course, this historic 1914 **lodge** (✆406-226-5600; www.glacierparkinc. com; r $169-256; ☺Jun-Sep; ☎☒) ✿ was built in the classic national park tradition with a splendid open-plan lobby supported by lofty 900-year-old Douglas fir timbers (imported from Washington state). Eye-catching Native American artwork adorns the communal areas, and a full-sized tipi is wedged incongruously onto a 2nd-floor balcony.

Top left: 'Jammer' bus; Top right: View along
Going-to-the-Sun Road; Bottom: St Mary Lake

TOP LEFT: SNEHIT/SHUTTERSTOCK ©; TOP RIGHT: PUNG/SHUTTERSTOCK ©

Traffic-Free Going-to-the-Sun Road

Imagine traveling up the mind-blowingly beautiful **Going-to-the-Sun Road** (www.nps.gov/glac/planyourvisit/goingtothesunroad.htm; ⊘mid-Jun–late Sep) with not a single car in sight. You can, but you have to work for it. While crews are plowing the pass in the spring, hikers and bicyclists can ride from Avalanche Creek toward Logan Pass as far as the road has been cleared. It's an excellent adventure that is becoming increasingly popular – but somehow we don't see too many bicycles ever being a problem.

Hike Hidden Lake Overlook Trail

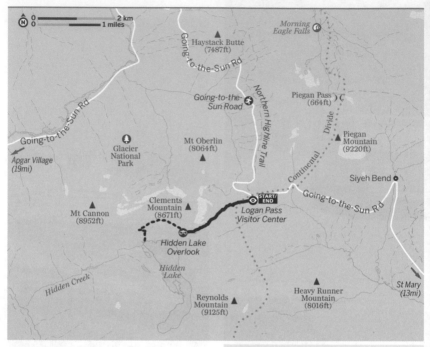

For many Glacier visitors this relatively straightforward hike is the one occasion when they step out of their cars and take a sniff of the sweet-scented alpine air for which the area is famous.

Starting at Logan Pass Visitor Center, the hike ascends gradually along a raised boardwalk (with steps) through expansive alpine meadows replete with monkeyflower and pink laurel. Slippery melting snowfields might add a challenge, but, rain or shine, this trail is a hit with everyone.

After about 0.6 miles, the boardwalk gives way to a gravel-dirt path. If the snow has melted, the diversity of grasses and wildflowers in the meadows around you is breathtaking. Resident trees include Engelmann spruce, subalpine fir and whitebark pine. Hoary marmots, ground squirrels and mountain goats are not shy along this trail. The elusive ptarmigan, whose brown feathers turn white in winter, also lives nearby.

Duration 2 hours round-trip

Distance 3 miles

Difficulty Easy–moderate

Elevation Change 494ft

Start & Finish Logan Pass Visitor Center

Nearest Town/Junction Logan Pass

Up-close mountain views include Clements Mountain to the north and Reynolds Mountain in the southeast.

About 300yd before the overlook, you will cross the Continental Divide – probably without realizing it – before your first stunning glimpse of the otherwordly, deep-blue **Hidden Lake**, bordered by mountain peaks and rocky cliffs. Look out for glistening Sperry Glacier visible to the south.

Hearty souls can continue on to Hidden Lake via a 1.5-mile trail from the overlook, steeply descending 765ft.

Hike Highline Trail

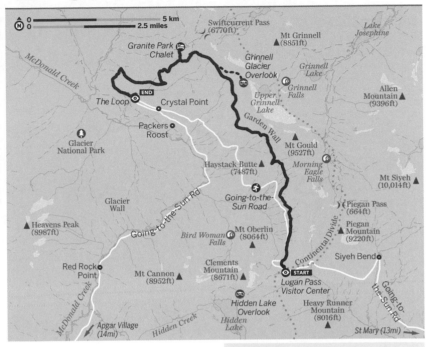

A Glacier classic, the Highline Trail cuts across the famous Garden Wall, a sharp, glacier-carved ridge that forms part of the Continental Divide.

Cutting immediately into the side of the mountain (a garden-hose-like rope is tethered to the rockwall for those with vertigo), the trail presents stunning early views of the Going-to-the-Sun Road and snow-capped Heavens Peak. Look out for the toy-sized red 'jammer' buses motoring up the valley below and the white foaming waters of 500ft **Bird Woman Falls** opposite.

After its vertiginous start, the trail is flat for 1.8 miles before gently ascending to a ridge that connects Haystack Butte with Mt Gould at the 3.5-mile mark. From here it's fairly flat as you bisect the mountainside on your way toward the Granite Park Chalet. After approximately 6.8 miles, with the chalet in sight, a spur path (on your right) offers the option of climbing up less than

Duration 7 hours one-way

Distance 11.6 miles

Difficulty Moderate

Elevation Change 830ft

Start Logan Pass Visitor Center

Finish The Loop

Nearest Town/Junction Logan Pass

1 mile to the **Grinnell Glacier Overlook** for a peek over the Continental Divide. The Granite Park Chalet appears at around 7.6 miles, providing a welcome haven for parched throats and tired feet.

From here you have three options: retrace your steps back to Logan Pass; head for Swiftcurrent Pass and the Many Glacier Valley; or descend 4 miles to the Loop, where you can pick up a shuttle bus to all points on the Going-to-the-Sun Road.

Hike Sun Point to Virginia Falls

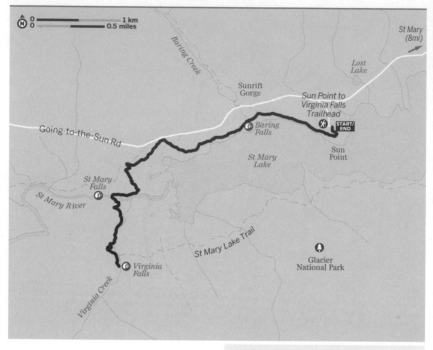

Handily served by the free park shuttle, the myriad trailheads along the eastern side of the Going-to-the-Sun Road offer plenty of short interlinking hikes, a number of which can be pooled together to make up a decent ramble.

Starting at the Sun Point shuttle stop, track down a 0.25-mile trail to a rocky (and often windy) **overlook** perched above St Mary Lake.

Take the path west through sun-flecked forest along the lake toward shady **Baring Falls**, at the 0.6-mile mark, for respite from the sun and/or wind. Cross the river and continue on the opposite bank to link up with the busy St Mary Falls Trail that joins from the right. Undemanding switchbacks lead up through the trees to the valley's

Duration 4 hours round-trip

Distance 7 miles

Difficulty Easy

Elevation Change 300ft

Start & Finish Sun Point shuttle stop

Nearest Town/Junction St Mary

most picturesque falls, set amid colorful foliage on St Mary River. Beyond, the trail branches along Virginia Creek, past a narrow gorge, to mist-shrouded **Virginia Falls** at the foot of a hanging valley.

Retrace your steps to Sun Point for the full-length hike or shortcut to St Mary Falls or Sunrift Gorge shuttle stops.

Drive Going-to-the-Sun Road

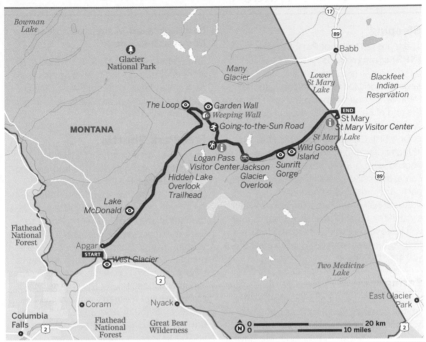

This is one of the most spectacular drives in the US. The road starts at Glacier NP's western entrance before tracking northeast along **Lake McDonald**. The valley here is lush, though a quick glance through the trees will show evidence of the 2003 Robert Fire on the opposite side of the water.

After following McDonald Creek for about 10 miles, the road begins its long, slow ascent to Logan Pass with a sharp turn to the southeast at the **Loop**, a famous hiking trailhead and the start of an increasingly precipitous climb toward the summit. Views here are unfailingly sublime as the road cuts precariously into the **Garden Wall**, an 8999ft granite ridge that delineates the west and east regions of the park along the Continental Divide. Look out for Bird Woman Falls, stunning even from a distance, and the more in-your-face **Weeping Wall**, as the gaping chasm to your right grows ever deeper.

Duration 3 hours (with stops)

Distance 53 miles

Start West Entrance, Apgar Village

Finish St Mary Visitor Center

Nearest Town/Junction West Glacier

Stop at lofty **Logan Pass** to browse the visitor center or to stretch your legs amid alpine meadows on the popular Hidden Lake Overlook Trail.

Descending eastwards, keep an eye out for majestic Going-to-the-Sun Mountain, to the north. At the 36-mile mark, you can pull over to spy one of only 25 remaining park glaciers at **Jackson Glacier Overlook**, while a few clicks further on, you can sample narrow **Sunrift Gorge** near the shores of St Mary Lake. **Wild Goose Island**, a photogenic stub of land, is situated in the center of the lake.

Essential Information

Sleeping

There are 13 **National Park Service (NPS) campgrounds** (☐518-885-3639; www.recreation.gov; tent & RV sites $10-23) and seven historic lodges in Glacier National Park, which operate between mid-May and the end of September. Lodges invariably require reservations.

Only Fish Creek, St Mary and a few sites at Many Glacier campgrounds can be booked in advance (up to five months). First-come, first served sites fill by mid-morning, particularly in July and August.

About half of the two to seven sites at each of the 65 backcountry campgrounds can be reserved; the rest are allotted on a first-come, first served basis the day before you start hiking.

Eating

In summer, there are grocery stores with limited camping supplies in Apgar, Lake McDonald Lodge, Rising Sun and at the Swiftcurrent Motor Inn. Most lodges have on-site restaurants. Dining options in West Glacier and St Mary offer mainly hearty hiking fare.

If cooking at a campground or picnic area, be sure to take appropriate bear-safety precautions and do not leave food unattended.

Orientation

Glacier's 1489 sq miles are divided into several regions, with distinct characters:

North Fork (northwest) A seldom-visited area with the isolated settlement of Polebridge.

Lake McDonald Valley (west) The park's largest lake has Apgar Village, Lake McDonald Lodge, and the west end of Going-to-the-Sun Road.

Two Medicine (southeast) A less-visited lake area that was once the center of east-side activity.

St Mary (east) The eastern end of Going-to-the-Sun Road has multiple hiking trails.

Many Glacier (northeast) Towering peaks box in a lake and the park's most dramatic lodge location.

Goat Haunt (north) A hikers' paradise accessible via boat from Canada.

The 50-mile Going-to-the-Sun Road (p149) is the only paved road that traverses the park while Hwy 2 connects West Glacier and East Glacier via the south boundary of the park.

Free Park Shuttle

See more with less stress by ditching the car and taking the park's free hop-on, hop-off **shuttle service** (www.nps.gov/glac/plan yourvisit/shuttles.htm; Apgar Visitor Center to St Mary Visitor Center; ☺9am-7pm Jul-Aug) 🏷FREE that hits all major points along Going-to-the-Sun Rd between Apgar and St Mary Visitor Centers. Buses run every 15 to 30 minutes depending on traffic, with the last trips down from Logan Pass leaving at 7pm.

Not only does taking the shuttle reduce emissions, but it means you can see the scenery instead of worrying about other drivers, and go hiking instead of trying to find parking at the trailheads.

Getting There & Away

Glacier Park International Airport (FCA; ☐406-257-5994; www.iflyglacier.com; 4170 Hwy 2 East) in Kalispell has year-round service to Salt Lake, Minneapolis, Denver, Seattle and Las Vegas, and seasonal service to Atlanta, Oakland, LA, Chicago and Portland.

The **Glacier Park Express** (☐406-253-9192; www.bigmtncommercial.org; Whitefish Library; adult/child round-trip $10/5; ☺Jul-early Sep) shuttle connects Whitefish to West Glacier.

Amtrak's *Empire Builder* stops daily at **West Glacier** (www.amtrak.com; ☺year-round) and **East Glacier Park** (☺Apr-Oct). Xanterra provides a shuttle ($10, 10 to 20 minutes) from West Glacier to its lodges on the west end, and Glacier Park, Inc. shuttles (from $15, one hour) connect East Glacier Park to St Mary. ∎

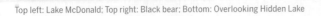

Top left: Lake McDonald; Top right: Black bear; Bottom: Overlooking Hidden Lake

RJRF STOCK/SHUTTERSTOCK ©

Snake River

Grand Teton National Park

Awesome in their grandeur, the Tetons have captivated the imagination from the moment humans laid eyes on them. This wilderness is home to bear, moose and elk in number, and played a fundamental role in the history of American alpine climbing.

Great For...

State
Wyoming

Entrance Fee
7-day pass per vehicle/pedestrian $35/20

Area
484 sq miles

❶ Climbing Grand Teton

The crowning glory of the park, dagger-edged Grand Teton (13,770ft) has taunted many a would-be mountaineer. The first white people to claim to have summited were James Stevenson and Nathanial Langford, part of the 1872 Hayden Geological Survey. However, when William Owen, Franklin Spalding and two others arrived at the top in 1898, they found no evidence of a prior expedition. So they chiseled their names in a boulder, claimed the first ascent, and ignited a dispute that persists today.

Today, climbers speckle the mountain's multiple routes throughout the summer season, and even very fit nonclimbers can reach the summit with a little training and a competent guide. The most popular route requires a combination of scrambling, easy 5th-class climbing and a few rappels, but should not be taken lightly. The park rescues 15 to 20 people a year, and fatalities are not uncommon.

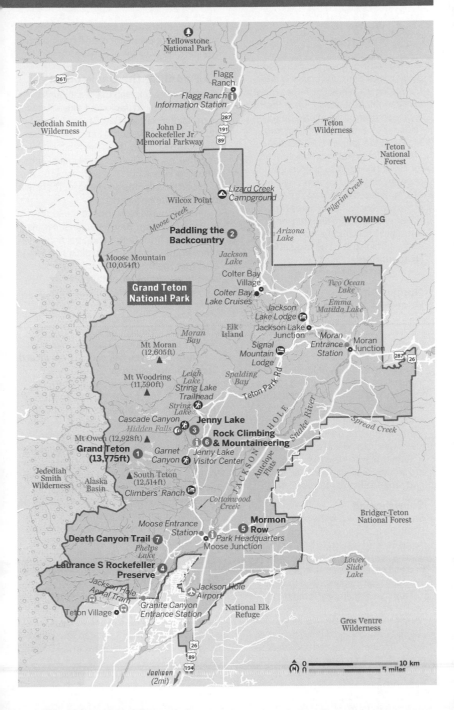

Yellowstone
National Park

Flagg
Ranch

*Flagg Ranch
Information Station*

261

John D
Rockefeller Jr
Memorial Parkway

287
191
89

Teton
Wilderness

Teton
National
Forest

Jedediah Smith
Wilderness

Lizard Creek
Campground

Wilcox Point

Moose Creek

Pilgrim Creek

WYOMING

Paddling the ② Backcountry

*Arizona
Lake*

▲ Moose Mountain
(10,054ft)

*Jackson
Lake*

Colter Bay
Village

*Two Ocean
Lake*

**Grand Teton
National Park**

Colter Bay ●
Lake Cruises

Elk
Island

*Jackson
Lake Lodge*

*Emma
Matilda Lake*

*Moran
Bay*

Mt Moran ▲
(12,605ft)

*Jackson
Lake
Junction*

*Signal
Mountain
Lodge*

Moran
Entrance
Station

Moran
Junction

Mt Woodring ▲
(11,590ft)

*Leigh
Lake*

String Lake
Trailhead

*Spalding
Bay*

*String
Lake*

287
26

Teton Park Rd

Cascade Canyon

Jenny Lake

Hidden Falls ③

Snake River

Mt Owen (12,928ft) ▲

**Grand Teton ①
(13,775ft)**

*Garnet
Canyon*

**Rock Climbing
& Mountaineering**

① ⑥

Jenny Lake
Visitor Center

J A C K S O N   H O L E

Spread Creek

Jedediah
Smith
Wilderness

Alaska
Basin

▲ South Teton
(12,514ft)

Climbers' Ranch

*Antelope
Flats*

Bridger-Teton
National Forest

*Cottonwood
Creek*

**Mormon ⑤
Row**

Moose Entrance
Station

Death Canyon Trail ⑦

*Phelps
Lake*

Park Headquarters
Moose Junction

**Laurance S Rockefeller
Preserve ④**

*Lower
Slide
Lake*

Jackson Hole
Aerial Tram

Jackson Hole
Airport

Teton Village ●

Granite Canyon
Entrance Station

National Elk
Refuge

Gros Ventre
Wilderness

26
89
194

*Jackson
(2mi)*

0 ————— 10 km
0 ————— 5 miles

Winter Activities

With the crowds gone, bears tucked away in their dens and powdery snow blanketing the pines, the Tetons make a lovely winter destination. Teton Park Rd is plowed from Jackson Lake Junction to Signal Mountain Lodge and from Moose to the Taggart Lake Trailhead.

Grand Teton National Park brochures for Nordic skiing (also appropriate for snowshoeing) and snowmobiling can be downloaded from www.nps.gov/grte/planyourvisit/brochures.htm.

Permits (free) are required for all overnight backcountry trips. Get one at the administration building at **Park Headquarters** (☑307-739-3300; ⊗9am-4:30pm Mon-Fri) in Moose.

Nordic Skiing

Between mid- December and mid-March, the park grooms 15 miles of track right under the Tetons' highest peaks, between the Taggart and Bradley Lakes parking area and Signal Mountain. Lanes are available for ski touring, skate skiing and snowshoeing. Grooming takes place two or three times per week. The NPS does not always mark every trail: consult at the ranger station to make sure that the trail you plan to use is well tracked and easy to follow.

Remember to yield to passing skiers and those skiing downhill. You can find rental equipment in Jackson.

Snowshoeing

Snowshoers may use the park's Nordic skiing trails. For an easy outing, try Teton Park Rd (closed to traffic in winter). Remember to use the hardpack trail and never walk on ski trails – skiers will thank you for preserving the track!

From late December through to mid-March, naturalists lead free two-hour, 1.5-mile snowshoe hikes from the Taggart Lake trailhead three times per week. Traditional wooden snowshoes are available for rental (adult/child $5/2). The tour is open to eight-year-olds and up.

Day climbers don't need to register, but those staying overnight need a backcountry-use permit (available at park visitor centers).

❷ Paddling the Backcountry

Overnight boaters can use backcountry campsites around **Jackson Lake** at Deadman Point, Bearpaw Bay, Grassy Island, Little Mackinaw Bay, South Landing, Elk Island and Warm Springs. Book these sites in advance, especially on summer weekends, when the lake is bursting with powerboats, sailboards, sailboats and canoes. There is a maximum three-night stay.

With dramatic close-ups of the toothy Mt Moran, **Moran Bay** is the most popular destination from Colter and Spalding Bays. While boating you can stop at Grassy Island en route. The following sample distances start from **Signal Mountain Marina** (☑307-543-2831; www.signalmountainlodge.com; ⊗7am-7:30pm mid-May–mid-Sep): Hermitage Point (2 miles), Elk Island (3 miles) and Grassy Island (6 miles); from Colter Bay to Little Mackinaw Bay it's 1.5 miles.

Alternatively, you can paddle from **Lizard Creek Campground** (☑800-672-6012; www.signalmountainlodge.com; off N Park Rd; sites $30; ⊗mid-Jun–early Sep) to remote backcountry trails on Jackson's northwest shore. Wilcox Point backcountry campsite (1.25 miles from Lizard Creek) provides backcountry access to Webb Canyon along the Moose Basin Divide Trail (20 miles). For a longer intermediate-level trip, paddle the twists and turns of the **Snake River** from Flagg Ranch to Wilcox Point or Lizard Creek.

Predominant winds from the southwest can be strong, especially in the afternoon, when waves can swamp canoes. Morning is usually the best time to paddle.

❸ Jenny Lake

The scenic heart of the Grand Tetons and the epicenter of the area's crowds, Jenny Lake was named for the Shoshone wife of early guide and mountain man Beaver Dick Leigh. Jenny died of smallpox in 1876 along with her children.

The **Jenny Lake Visitor Center** (☑307-739-3343; Teton Park Rd; ⊗8am-4:30pm

Sep-May, to 7pm Jun-Aug) is worth a visit for its geological displays and 3D map of Jackson Hole. The cabin was once in a different location as the Crandall photo studio.

The Jenny Lake area has completed a massive $19 million restoration to trails and infrastructure. The five-year project was unveiled in 2019.

From the visitor center, a network of trails leads clockwise around the lake for 2.5 miles to **Hidden Falls** and then continues for a short uphill run to fine views at **Inspiration Point**. Once you're here, it's worth continuing up **Cascade Canyon** with a good supply of water for more excellent views. From here, you can return the way you came or continue clockwise 1.5 miles to the **String Lake Trailhead** to make a 3.8-mile circle around the lake. If you're walking the Jenny Lake Trail in the early morning or late afternoon, detour approximately 15 minutes (about 0.5 miles) from the visitor center to **Moose Ponds** for a good chance of spotting moose.

Alternatively, **Jenny Lake Boating** (📞307-734-9227; www.jennylakeboating.com; round-trip shuttle adult/child 2-11yr $15/8, scenic cruise $19/11; ⏱7am-7pm Jun-late Sep) runs shuttles across Jenny Lake between the east-shore boat dock near Jenny Lake Visitor Center and the west-shore dock near Hidden Falls, offering quick (12-minute) access to Inspiration Point and the Cascade Canyon Trail. Shuttles run every 15 minutes, but expect long waits for return shuttles between 4pm and 6pm.

❹ Laurance S Rockefeller Preserve

For solitude coupled with the most stunning views that don't include the Grand, visitors should check out this newer section of Grand Teton National Park. Once the JY Ranch, an exclusive Rockefeller family retreat, these 3100 acres around Phelps Lake were donated in full by Laurance S Rockefeller in 2001. His grandfather, John D Rockefeller, had been an early park advocate, purchasing the first tracts of land to donate in 1927. Despite strong local opposition, by 1949 he had donated some 33,000 acres of former ranchland to Grand Teton National Park.

Jenny Lake

KRISHNA WU/SHUTTERSTOCK ©

With this sector, Laurance Rockefeller's vision was to create a space of refuge and renewal. In contrast to other visitor centers, the beautiful **Laurance S Rockefeller Preserve Center** (☎307-739-3654; www.nps.gov/grte/planyourvisit/lsrpvc.htm; Moose–Wilson Rd; ⊙9am-5pm Jun-Sep) ✐ is a meditative experience. Sparely furnished and certified by LEED (Leadership in Energy and Environmental Design), the green building features quotes from naturalists and writers etched into walls, giant picture windows to admire the views, and a library with leather armchairs and books on conservation and nature to browse. The center also hosts a full menu of ranger programs.

❺ Mormon Row

This is possibly the most photographed spot in the park – and for good reason. The aged wooden barns and fence rails make a quintessential pastoral scene, perfectly framed by the imposing bulk of the Tetons. The barns and houses were built in the 1890s by Mormon settlers, who farmed the fertile alluvial soil irrigated by miles of hand-dug ditches.

Top: Hikers in Grand Teton; Bottom: Death Canyon

Just north of Moose Junction, head east on Antelope Flats Rd for 1.5 miles to a three-way intersection and parking area. Landmark buildings are north and south of the intersection.

❻ Rock Climbing & Mountaineering

The Tetons are known for excellent short-route rock climbs, as well as classic longer routes to summits such as Grant Teton, Mt Moran and Mt Owen (12,928ft), all best attempted with an experienced guide.

Jenny Lake Ranger Station (☎307-739-3343; off Teton Park Rd, South Jenny Lake Junction; ⊗8am-6pm Jun-Aug) is the go-to office for climbing information. It sells climbing guidebooks, provides information and has a board showing campsite availability in **Garnet Canyon**, the gateway to climbs including the technical ascent of Grand Teton.

An excellent resource and the spot to meet outdoor partners in crime, the member-supported American Alpine Club's **Climbers' Ranch** (☎307-733-7271; www.americanalpineclub.org/grand-teton-climbers-ranch; End Highlands Rd; dm $27; ⊗Jun-Sep) has been a climbing institution since 1970. It also offers lodging.

❼ Death Canyon Trail

Death Canyon is one of our favorite hikes – both for the challenge and the astounding scenery. The trail ascends a mile to the Phelps Lake overlook before dropping down into the valley bottom and following Death Canyon.

For a tougher add-on with impossibly beautiful views, turn right at the historic ranger cabin onto the Alaska Basin Trail and climb another 3000ft to Static Peak Divide (10,792ft) – the highest trail in Grand Teton National Park.

Drive Hole-in-One

PAUL BRADY PHOTOGRAPHY/SHUTTERSTOCK ©

A scenic drive through sagebrush flats and forest with picturesque barns and Teton panoramas.

Duration 1 hour plus stops

Distance 40-mile loop

Start & Finish Jackson

You could say Gros Ventre Butte ruined it for Jackson – there are no Teton views from the park's main hub due to the blockage created by this hump. But this driving tour, not suitable for RVs or other oversize vehicles, is just the remedy.

Head out of Jackson on Hwy 191. First stop: the **National Museum of Wildlife Art** (☎307-733-5771; www.wildlifeart.org; 2820 Rungius Road; adult/child $14/6; ☺9am-5pm daily May-Oct, reduced hours rest of year). You may ask, why do this when you have the real thing? Just look. The way these masters envisioned this landscape will change the way you see it yourself.

Continue north on Hwy 191. At the Gros Ventre Junction, take a right and drive along Gros Ventre Rd, skirting the **Gros Ventre River**, lined with cottonwoods, juniper, spruce and willows. The river ecology contrasts sharply with the dry sagebrush flats to its north, where pronghorn can often be seen, bounding at speeds up to 60mph. At the next junction, take a left onto Antelope Flats Rd to drive north on **Mormon Row**, a picturesque strip that includes a much-photographed rambling barn (pictured). At the end of the row, loop left on **Antelope Flats Road**, where bison and pronghorn roam the grasslands. It soon meets Hwy 191: go left, then right at Moose Junction.

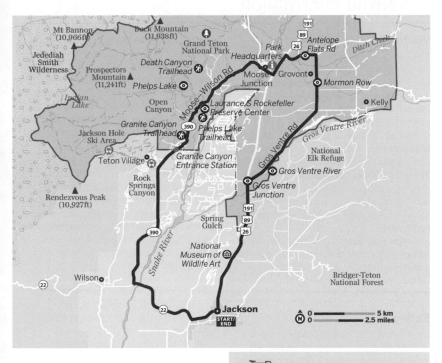

Before the park entrance gate, take a left onto narrow **Moose–Wilson Road**. You will need to squeeze onto the shoulder for oncoming traffic: this is why oversize vehicles are explicitly banned. Mind the blind curves, twisting through dense foliage. You will pass turnoffs for Death Canyon trailhead, Phelps Lake trailhead (near the Laurance S Rockefeller Preserve Center) and Granite Canyon trailhead. If you're keen on a swim, these trails will take you to **Phelps Lake**; it's a 30- to 45-minute walk along the Woodland Trail from Phelps Lake trailhead. This short section of the road is unpaved but even.

The road spills out near **Teton Village**, where you can take a gondola (p163) to the top for views or grab lunch. Follow the Moose–Wilson Rd south to Hwy 22. Go left to return to Jackson.

🚲 Cycle Hole-in-One

Duration 5 hours

Distance 33-mile loop

Difficulty Moderate

Elevation Change 340ft

Start in Jackson and head north on Hwy 191 to **Moose Junction**. Go left here and left again to the narrow and winding Moose–Wilson Rd. While it is paved, there are some deep potholes, so stay alert. Horned owls nest along this section.

Approaching **Teton Village**, the road becomes smooth and stays that way. Continue on the flats of Moose–Wilson Rd until you hit a junction with Hwy 22; turn left here for Jackson. There will be a lot of car traffic on Hwy 22.

An early start will help you avoid traffic on the narrows of Moose–Wilson Rd.

Essential Information

Visitor Service Hubs

The park's southern hub is **Moose**, with a visitor center, a gas station, accommodations, restaurants, groceries and equipment rental. The nearby Laurance S Rockefeller Preserve Center (p156) is south on the Moose–Wilson Rd.

Further north on Teton Park Rd, **Signal Mountain** has accommodations, a grocery store, a gas station and a restaurant. North of here, **Jackson Lake Lodge** (307-543-3100; www.gtlc.com/lodges/jackson-lake-lodge; Jackson Lake Lodge Rd; r & cottages $330-449; mid-May–early Oct;) has shops and restaurants.

Colter Bay hosts the highest concentration of visitor services, with a visitor center, gas station, grocery store, restaurants, laundromat, showers, campground, RV park and marina.

Eating

There's fast food, basic markets and even upscale dining in the park. Other options include taking a Jackson Lake dinner or breakfast **cruise** (307-543-2811; www.gtlc.com/activities/jackson-lake-boat-cruises; Colter Bay Marina; cruise adult/child 3-11yr $34/14; late May-late Sep) or packing a picnic basket. **Dornan's Trading Post** (307-733-2415; www.dornans.com; 8am-8pm) in Moose offers an impressive selection of wines. Campground diners must store food in bear-proof boxes or cars – never leave it unattended and always dispose of food properly.

Getting There & Away

Jackson Hole Airport (JAC; 307-733-7682; www.jacksonholeairport.com; 1250 E Airport Rd) lies inside the park's boundaries and sees a steady stream of traffic. Currently, there is no regular shuttle service through the park, though several companies in Jackson provide guided tours.

The park begins 4.5 miles north of Jackson. There are three entrance stations. The easiest to access from Jackson is the

Moose Entrance Station (South Entrance; Teton Park Rd; hours vary), west of Moose Junction. From Teton Village, the **Granite Canyon Entrance Station** (Southwest Entrance; Moose-Wilson Rd; hours vary) is a mile or so north. If driving south from Yellowstone, enter via the **Moran Entrance** (North Entrance; Hwy 287; hours vary), just north of Moran Junction.

Sleeping

Camping inside the park is permitted in designated campgrounds only and is limited to 14 days (seven days at popular Jenny Lake). The NPS operates the park's six campgrounds (www.nps.gov/grte/planyourvisit/camping.htm) on a first-come, first-served basis.

Demand for campsites is highest from early July to Labor Day, and most campgrounds fill by 11am (checkout time). Jenny Lake fills by about 8am; Gros Ventre fills later, if at all.

Signal Mountain is a popular base because of its central location. Colter Bay, Jenny Lake, Lizard Creek and Signal Mountain have tent-only sites reserved for walk-in hikers and ride-in cyclists ($11 to $12).

Lodging should be reserved as far in advance as possible, especially for peak-season dates. Grand Teton Lodge Company accepts reservations for the following season starting November 1. Most campgrounds are first-come, first-served but some allow a limited number of reservations. See websites for details.

The park's concessionaires:

Grand Teton Lodge Company (GTLC; 307-543-3100; www.gtlc.com)

Spur Ranch Log Cabins (307-733-2522; www.dornans.com; Moose; cabins $250-350; closed Nov & Apr)

Signal Mountain Lodge (307-543-2831; www.signalmtnlodge.com; Teton Park Rd; r $262-368, cabins $218-278, ste $367-408; early May–mid-Oct;)

Top left: Antelope Flats; Top right: Bald eagle; Bottom: Signal Mountain Lodge

CLASSIC HIKES

Teton Crest Trail

This classic route is one to remember. Dipping in and out of the neighboring Jedediah Smith Wilderness, the trail has numerous routes out – namely the canyons and passes that access it on either side. Hikers must arrange for a shuttle or have two cars to leave at the start and end points.

Duration 4 or 5 days

Distance 31.4 or 39.9 miles

Difficulty Moderate–difficult

Start String Lake trailhead

Finish Granite Canyon trailhead or Teton Village

Nearest Town/Junction North Jenny Lake Junction

DAY 1: String Lake trailhead to Holly Lake (5 hours, 6.2 miles)

From the String Lake parking lot, take the trail that curves south around String Lake. It climbs gently until the left-hand junction with Paintbrush Canyon, 1.6 miles in. This steep but moderate trail borders a stream flowing over granite boulders, passing through the Lower Paintbrush Camping Zone and some stock campsites. It climbs ever higher to reach an upper basin surrounded by snowy peaks. The first lake is unnamed; continue right of it to reach

Holly Lake (9424ft). There are two good shady designated campsites at the lake's southeast corner. If these sites are booked, camp in the Upper Paintbrush Canyon Camping Zone. For a great day hike, you can return via the same route (12.4 miles, 7 hours total), enjoying the lake views framed by the valley above.

DAY 2: Holly Lake to South Fork Cascade Camping Zone (time varies with conditions, 6.6 miles)

Day two takes you over a scree field to Paintbrush Divide. This section with loose boulders can be sketchy, so take it very slowly. Ice tools may be necessary, so check with rangers on conditions before heading out. Follow the divide down switchbacks to Lake Solitude (9035ft), until the Forks junction between the North and South Forks of Cascade Canyon. Here the trail branches up the South Fork to the South Fork Cascade Camping Zone (19 campsites).

Alternatively, you can start the hike from Jenny Lake, catching a boat shuttle across the lake to Inspiration Point and hiking up Cascade Creek Trail to spend the first night at the South Fork Cascade Camping Zone. With the boat shuttle, this 10.4-mile hike (2050ft elevation gain) shaves off a day. The hike may be longer, depending on your assigned campsite. Allow a minimum of seven hours.

DAY 3: South Fork Cascade Camping Zone to Alaska Basin (3–3½ hours, 6.1 miles)

The trail climbs up to **Avalanche Divide** junction: head right (southwest) to **Hurricane Pass** (10,372ft), which has unsurpassed views of the Grand, South and Middle Tetons. (An excursion from the Avalanche Divide junction leads 1.6 miles to the divide, a scenic overlook above Snowdrift Lake.) From the pass, the trail descends into the Jedediah Smith Wilderness, past

Sunset Lake, into the **Basin Lakes** of the Alaska Basin, where you'll find several popular campsites. No permits are needed here since you're outside the park, but you must camp at least 200ft from lakes and 150ft from streams.

DAY 4: Alaska Basin to Marion Lake (4½ hours, 8.2 miles)

The trail crosses South Fork Teton Creek on stepping stones and switchbacks up the Sheep Steps to the wide saddle of **Mt Meek Pass** (9718ft) to reenter the park. For the next 3 miles, the trail dips into the stunning plateau of **Death Canyon Shelf** and the camping zone. Past the turnoff to Death Canyon, it climbs to **Fox Creek Pass** (9560ft) and continues southwest over a vague saddle to **Marion Lake** and its designated campsites.

DAY 5: Marion Lake to Teton Village via Tram (5 hours, 6.5 miles to tram top)

The trail descends into the Upper Granite Canyon Camping Zone and continues past the Upper Granite Canyon patrol cabin to the junction with the Valley Trail. From here, head southeast to Teton Village, ascending the back side of the resort to take the **Jackson Hole Aerial Tram** (📞307-733-2292; adult/child $43/28, mountain-biking pass $37, descent free; ⊙9am-5pm mid-May–early Oct), or continue east to the Granite Canyon trailhead (10.3 miles total). ∎

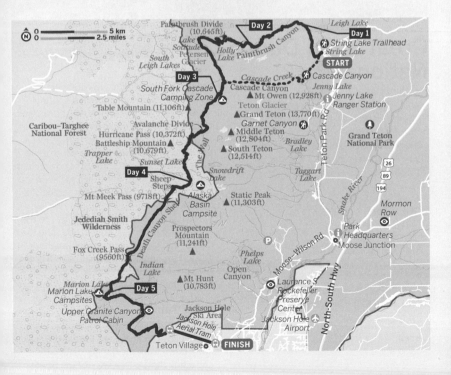

GALYNA ANDRUSHKO/SHUTTERSTOCK ©

Great Sand Dunes National Park

For all of Colorado's striking natural sights, the surreal Great Sand Dunes National Park, a veritable sea of sand bounded by jagged peaks and scrubby plains, is a place of stirring optical illusions where nature's magic is on full display.

Great For...

🚲 🏞️ 🥾

State
Colorado

Entrance Fee
7-day pass per vehicle $20

Area
55 sq miles

From the approach up Hwy 150, watch as the angles of sunlight make shifting shadows on the dunes; the most dramatic time is the day's end, when the hills come into high contrast as the sun drops low on the horizon. Hike past the edge of the dune field to see the shifting sand up close; the ceaseless wind works like a disconsolate sculptor, constantly amending the landscape.

Most visitors limit their activities to the area where Medano Creek divides the main dune mass from the towering Sangre de Cristo Mountains. The remaining 85% of the park's area is designated wilderness: not for the unfit or fainthearted.

Inner Tubing

One of the most curious spectacles in the entire park, the snowmelt **Medano Creek** flows down from the Sangre de Cristos and along the eastern edge of the dunes. Peak flow is usually in late May or early

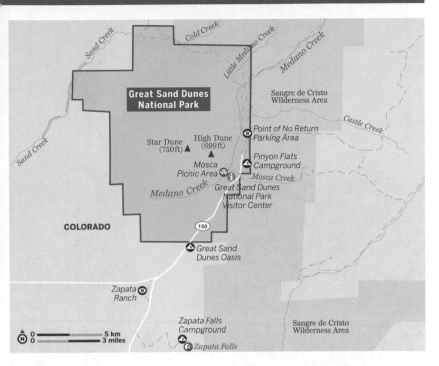

June, and the rippling water over the sand creates a temporary beach of sorts, which is extremely popular with families. In years when the water is high enough (check the park website for daily water-level reports; the level of late has been very low), children can even float down the creek on an inner tube, right along the dunes. The combination of the creek's appeal and the end of the school year means that this is the park's peak season.

Hiking

There are no trails through this expansive field of sand, but it's the star attraction for hikers. Two informal hikes afford excellent panoramic views of the dunes. The first is a hike to **High Dune** (699ft; strangely, not the highest dune in the park), which departs from a parking area just beyond the visitor center. It's about 2.5 miles out to the peak and back, but be warned: it's not easy. As you trudge along up the hills of sand, it feels like you're taking a half-step

back for every one forward. If you're up for it, try pushing on to the second worthy goal: just west of High Dune is **Star Dune** (755ft), the tallest in the park.

From the Great Sand Dunes National Park Visitor Center (p168), a short trail leads to the **Mosca Picnic Area** next to ankle-deep Medano Creek, which you must ford (when the creek is running) to reach the dunes. Across the road from the visitor center, the **Mosca Pass Trail** climbs up into the Sangre de Cristo Wilderness.

The area beyond the Point of No Return parking lot is a good spot to get further out into the backcountry on backpacking trips; a road theoretically leads up to Medano Pass (9982ft) at the top of the Sangres, but because of the sand it's not recommended unless you have a suitable off-road vehicle.

In the middle of summer, hikers should hit the hills during the early morning, as the sand can reach 140°F (60°C) during the heat of the day. Although you might think sandals would be the footwear of choice,

Zapata Falls

closed-toe shoes provide better protection against the heat. Those with limited mobility can borrow a dunes-accessible wheelchair from the visitor center. If you are hiking with children, don't let them out of your sight. It is very easy to become separated once you've entered the dunes.

Dune Sandboarding & Sledding

The heavy wooden sled may seem like a bad idea when you're trudging out to the dunes, but the gleeful rush down the slopes is worth every footstep. There's a bit of a trick to making this work. Sand conditions are best after a recent precipitation; when it's too dry you'll simply sink. Also, the best rides are had by those who are relatively light, so if you've bulked up on microbrews and steaks, don't expect to zip down the hill.

During the winter days when snow covers the dunes, the sledding is excellent. To rent a board, visit **Kristi Mountain Sports** (☎719-589-9759; www.slvoutdoor.com; 3323 Main St; sandboard/bike rental per day $18/20; ☺9am-6pm Mon-Sat) in Alamosa or the **Great Sand Dunes Oasis** (☎719-378-2222; www.greatdunes.com; 5400 Hwy 150; tent/RV sites $25/38, cabins $55, r $100; ☺Apr-Oct; @) at the edge of the park.

Mountain Biking

Off-road cyclists should plan for a real slog. The unimproved roads of the park get washed over in sand and are very difficult until the road climbs the beautiful narrow valley to **Medano Pass**. The pass is 11 miles from the Point of No Return parking area at the north end of the paved road. A detailed mileage log for the Medano Pass Primitive Rd is available at the visitor center.

For a shorter fat-tire ride, visit the spectacular area around **Zapata Falls**, south of the park, which also offers outstanding views of the valley. A consortium of 13 agencies has opened 4 miles of trail in the Zapata Falls Special Recreation Area on the west flank of Blanca Peak.

Why All the Sand?

Upon your first glimpse of the dunes, you can't help but wonder: where did all this sand come from, and why does it stay here? Has it got something to do with the aliens you might spy from the **UFO Watchtower** (☎805-886-6959; www.ufowatchtower.com; Hwy 17; per person/car $2/5)?

The answer lies in the unique geography and weather patterns of the San Luis Valley. Streams, snowmelt and flash floods have been carrying eroded sand and silt out of the San Juan Mountains (about 60 miles to the west) to the valley floor for millions of years.

There, prevailing winds from the southwest gradually blow the sand into the natural hollow at the southern end of the Sangre de Cristo range. At the same time, streams and stronger prevailing winds from the eastern mountains push back in the other direction, causing the sand to pile up into what are now the highest dunes in North America.

If you look closely at the sand (the visitor center has a magnifying glass) you'll see a spectrum of shapes and colors: 29 different rock and mineral types – from obsidian and sulfur to amethyst and turquoise – are represented in the sand's makeup.

Guided Tours

Throughout summer NPS rangers lead interpretive nature walks from the visitor center and hold evening programs at the amphitheater. This is an excellent way to learn more about the unseen world of the dunes – surprising thickets of sunflowers, burrowing owls and even tiger salamanders! Inquire at the visitor center about specific programs and times.

Essential Information

Sleeping

For beauty at its spookiest, plan your visit during a full or new moon. Stock up on supplies, get your backcountry camping permit and hike into the surreal landscape to set up camp: bring plenty of shade and water.

There are also half-a-dozen backcountry sites that can be accessed from the Point of No Return parking lot, north of Pinyon Flats. These sites vary in terrain, from alpine and woodland to desert.

Tourist Information

Stop by the informative **Great Sand Dunes National Park Visitor Center** (📱719-378-6399; www.nps.gov/grsa; 11999 Hwy 150; 🕑8:30am-5pm Jun-Aug, 9am-4:30pm Sep-May) before venturing out, to learn about the geology and history of the dunes or to chat with a ranger about hiking or backcountry-camping options. A free backcountry permit is required if you're planning on being adventurous, and it pays to let the ranger know where you're going.

Be sure to ask about scheduled nature walks and nightly programs held at the amphitheater near Pinyon Flats.

Getting There & Away

Great Sand Dunes National Park is 33 miles northeast of Alamosa. To get here, travel east on US 160 for 14 miles toward prominent Blanca Peak, turn left (north) on Hwy 150 and follow the road for 19 miles to the visitor center, 3 miles north of the park entrance. You can also get here from the north, turning west off Hwy 17 onto County Lane 6 N. ∎

Top left: Visitor Center entrance; Top right: Sandboarding; Bottom: Medano Creek

Rocky Mountain National Park

This is a place of natural spectacle on every scale: from hulking granite formations, many taller than 12,000ft, some over 130 million years old, to the delicate yellow burst of the glacier lily, one of the dozen alpine wildflowers that explode in short, colorful life at the edge of receding snowfields every spring.

Great For...

State
Colorado

Entrance Fee
7-day pass per vehicle/person $35/20

Area
415 sq miles

Wonders of the natural world are the main attractions here: huge herds of elk and scattered bighorn sheep, pine-dotted granite slopes and blindingly white alpine tundra. However, there are a few museums and historic sites within the park's borders that are worthy of a glance and good for families.

Rocky Mountain National Park is surrounded by some of the most pristine wild area in the west: Comanche Peak and Neota Wilderness Areas in the Roosevelt National Forest to the north and Indian Peaks Wilderness to the south. The jagged spine of the Continental Divide intersects the park through its middle.

❶ Moraine Park Discovery Center

Built by the Civilian Conservation Corps in 1923 and once the park's proud visitors lodge, this **building** (☏970-586-1206; Bear Lake Rd; ⏲9am-4:30pm Jun-Oct) **FREE** has

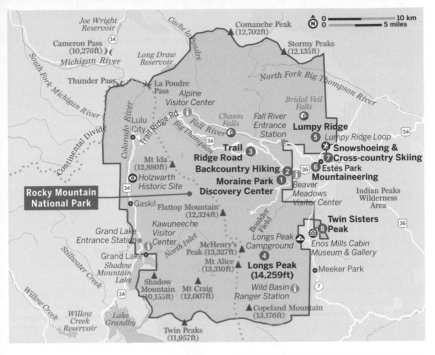

ANN MCCORE/SHUTTERSTOCK ©

Holzwarth Historic Site

When Prohibition was enacted in 1916, John Holzwarth Sr, a Denver saloonkeeper, started a new life as a subsistence rancher. This **site** (Never Summer Ranch; ☎park headquarters 970-586-1206; Trail Ridge Rd/US 34; ⊙10am-4pm Jun-Oct) houses several buildings kept in their original condition, including the 'Mama cabin' and cabins that were part of a dude ranch, which the Holzwarths rented out for $2 a day.

Historical reenactments and ranger-led programs are now held at the site. The **Heritage Days** celebration happens in late July.

Holzwarth (pictured left) lies at the end of a graded half-mile path, easily accessible with strollers.

**Cycling &
Mountain Biking**

Mountain biking and cycling have continued to gain popularity despite the park's heavy traffic. It's a splendid way to see the park and wildlife, though bicycle travel is restricted to paved roads and to one dirt road, Fall River Rd. Those looking to ride technical routes on a mountain bike should go to Roosevelt National Forest.

On either a road bike or a mountain bike, climbing the paved **Trail Ridge Rd** (www.nps.gov/romo; ⊙summer only) FREE has one big advantage over Fall River Rd (a 9-mile one-way climb of more than 3000ft): you can turn around should problems arise.

Less daunting climbs and climes are available on the park's lower paved roads. A popular 16-mile circuit is the Horseshoe Park/Estes Park Loop. For a bit more of a climbing challenge you can continue to Bear Lake Rd, an 8-mile-long route that rises 1500ft to the high mountain basin with a decent shoulder.

To avoid hypothermia and dehydration, bring a set of dry, long-sleeved clothes, plus plenty of water.

been renovated in recent years to host exhibits on geology, glaciers and wildlife. Kids will like the interactive exhibits and half-mile nature trail out the door.

❷ Backcountry Hiking

Most people never leave the road and major trails in Rocky Mountain National Park – and it's a damned shame. Luckily for you, this means the backcountry is a desolate paradise where you can find solitude, amazing views, wild hikes and serious mountain ascents. You'll need to get permits through the **Wilderness Offices** (☑970-586-1242; www.nps.gov/romo; 1000 W Hwy 36, Estes Park, CO 80517) before heading out.

Backcountry camping happens in designated sites throughout the park – there are over a hundred. This means the real opportunity of spending a few days without seeing anyone. You can move from site to site, or stay in one site for a few days, taking on day trips. Consider going to one of the Technical Orienteering Cross Country Zones to really get into the backcountry and enjoy trailless hiking across the lost corners of the park. You will need at the minimum: a permit, a bear bin, proper clothing, a map and compass, food, a tent, a sleeping bag and pad, good shoes and water filtration. Remember to keep bear-safe camps and watch for falling trees in areas where blight is killing off pines.

❸ Trail Ridge Road

Travel through the sky on this remarkable 48-mile road between Estes Park and Grand Lake. The road is only open summers, and can be jam-packed. But it is really worth it – by car, RV or bicycle. About 11 miles of the road sit above the tree line.

Along the way, you might sight elk, moose, marmots and plenty of birds and plant species.

❹ Longs Peak

You need not worry about getting lonesome on the 15-mile (full-day) round-trip to Longs Peak (14,259ft) summit, as it's the centerpiece of many a hiker's itinerary. During summer, you're likely to find a line of more than 100 parked cars snaking down the road from the Longs Peak trailhead.

This is a serious climb, and you should be prepared before taking it on. After the initial 6 miles of moderate trail to the Boulder Field (12,760ft), the path steepens at the start of the **Keyhole Route** to the summit, which is marked with yellow-and-red bull's-eyes painted on the rock (while there are dozens of ways up, this is the easiest). Even superhuman athletes who are used to the thin air will be slowed by the route's ledge system, which resembles a narrow cliffside stairway without a handrail. After this, hikers scramble the final homestretch to the summit boulders. The view from the top – snow-kissed granite stretching out to the curved horizon – is incredible. The round-trip hike takes anywhere from 10 to 15 hours. The rule in Colorado is you need to hit the summit before noon to avoid lightning storms, so expect to make an early alpine start.

For a shorter hike, head south just above the tree line to make it to **Chasm Lake**, a high-alpine wonder that sits below the jagged face of Longs Peak's signature **Diamond**, where heavy-duty rock gods and goddesses test their mettle.

Overnighting at **Longs Peak Campground** (970-586-1206; Longs Peak Rd, off State Hwy 7; tent sites $26; closed winter) is a good idea.

⑤ Lumpy Ridge

Easily accessed from the north side of Estes Park, Lumpy Ridge offers some great hikes to places like Bridal Veil Falls and Gem Lake, plus some of the best rock climbing in the area. The **Lumpy Ridge Loop** circles around the granite crag in an 11-mile loop. Check in about raptor nesting before going here.

Rock climbing here is focused on traditional crack climbing. Expect solid granite, great views and accessional crowds.

⑥ Mountaineering

Rocky Mountain National Park has a total 124 named peaks. While Longs is the only one over 14,000ft, another 20 sit above 13,000ft, making this a top mountaineering spot. Before departing check in at wilderness offices (p172) for raptor closings as well as beta on climbing and bivouac permits.

Routes range from easy hikes up to day-long affairs on vertical cliffs, plus steep snow, ice and rock routes. Take classes at the **Colorado Mountain School** (720-387-8944; https://coloradomountainschool. com; 341 Moraine Ave; half-day guided climbs per person from $150).

View from Trail Ridge Road

❼ Snowshoeing & Cross-country Skiing

From December into May, the high valleys and alpine tundra offer cross-country skiers unique opportunities to view wildlife and the winter scenery undisturbed by crowds. January and February are the best months for dry, powdery snowpack; spring snows tend to be heavy and wet. Most routes follow summer hiking trails, but valley bottoms and frozen streambeds typically have more snow cover and are less challenging. Ask about avalanche hazards before heading out – Colorado has one of the most dangerous snowpacks in the world with people dying in slides most years – and avoid steep, open slopes.

Novices should consider hiring a guide or traveling with experienced leaders. Rangers lead weekend snowshoe hikes in the east side of the park from January to April, depending on snow conditions. Trailhead locations and times are available from the park visitor centers.

Overnight trips require permits, and the US Forest Service (USFS) and NPS will have a list of closed trails.

You can gear up at the **Estes Park Mountain Shop** (☑970-586-6548; www. estesparkmountainshop.com; 2050 Big Thompson Ave; 2-person tents $12-16, bear boxes per night $3; ⊙8am-9pm).

❽ Twin Sisters Peak

This up-and-back hike provides an excellent warm-up to climbing Longs Peak. In addition, the 11,428ft summit of Twin Sisters Peak offers unequaled views of Longs Peak. It's an arduous walk, gaining 2300ft in just 3.7 miles.

Erosion-resistant quartz rock caps the oddly deformed rock at the summit and delicate alpine flowers (plenty of mountain harebell) fill the rock spaces near the summit's stone hut. The trailhead is near Mills Cabin, 10 miles south of Estes Park on Hwy 7.

Essential Information

Camping

The park's formal campgrounds provide campfire programs, have public telephones and a seven-day limit during summer months; all except Longs Peak (p172) take RVs (no hookups). The water supply is turned off during winter.

You will need a **backcountry permit** (www.nps.gov/romo/planyourvisit/wilderness-camping.htm; permit for up to 7 people $26) to stay outside developed park campgrounds. None of the campgrounds have showers, but they do have flush toilets in summer and outhouse facilities in winter. Sites include a fire ring, a picnic table and one parking spot. Most have bear boxes for food storage.

Getting There & Around

Trail Ridge Rd (US 34) is the only east–west route through the park; the US 34 eastern approach from I-25 and Loveland follows the Big Thompson River Canyon. The most direct route from Boulder follows US 36 through Lyons to the east entrances. Another approach from the south, mountainous Hwy 7, passes by **Enos Mills Cabin** (970-586-4706; www.enosmills.com; 6760 Hwy 7; $20; 11am-4pm Tue & Wed summer, by appointment only) and provides access to campsites and trailheads on the east side of the divide. Winter closure of US 34 through the park makes access to the park's west side dependent on US 40 at Granby.

A majority of visitors enter the park in their own cars, using the long and winding Trail Ridge Rd (US 34) to cross the Continental Divide. There are options for those without wheels, however. In summer a free shuttle bus operates from the **Estes Park Visitor Center** (970-577-9900; www.visit estespark.com; 500 Big Thompson Ave; 9am-8pm daily Jun-Aug, 8am-5pm Mon-Fri, 9am-5pm Sat, 10am-4pm Sun Sep-May) multiple times daily, bringing hikers to a park-and-ride location where they can pick up other shuttles. The year-round option leaves the Glacier Basin parking area and heads to Bear Lake, in the park's lower elevations. During the summer peak, a second shuttle operates between Moraine Park campground and the Glacier Basin parking area. The second shuttle runs on weekends only from mid-August through September.

Information

The park has three full-service visitor centers – one on the east side, one on the west and one in the middle. Though they all have different displays and programs, this is where you can study maps and speak with rangers about permits and weather conditions.

Alpine Visitor Center (www.nps.gov/romo; Fall River Pass; 10:30am-4:30pm late May–mid-Jun, 9am-5pm late Jun-early Sep, 10:30am-4:30pm early Sep–mid-Oct) The views from this popular visitor center and souvenir store at 11,796ft, and right in the middle of the park, are extraordinary. You can see elk, deer and sometimes moose grazing on the hillside on the drive up Old Fall River Rd. Much of the traffic that clogs Trail Ridge Rd all summer pulls into Alpine Visitor Center, so the place is a zoo. Rangers here give programs and advice about trails. You can also shop for knickknacks or eat in the cafeteria-style dining room.

Beaver Meadows Visitor Center (970-586-1206; www.nps.gov/romo; US Hwy 36; 8am-9pm late Jun-late Aug, to 4:30pm or 5pm rest of year) The primary visitor center and best stop for park information if you're approaching from Estes Park. You can see a film about the park, browse a small gift shop and reserve backcountry camping sites.

Kawuneeche Visitor Center (970-627-3471; 16018 US Hwy 34; 8am-6pm last week May–Labor Day, to 5pm Labor Day–Sep, to 4:30pm Oct-May) This visitor center is on the west side of the park, and offers a film about the park, ranger-led walks and discussions, backcountry permits and family activities. ∎

Top left: Mule deer; Top right: Cross-country skiing; Bottom: Waterfall

Bison in the Lamar Valley

Yellowstone National Park

Yellowstone National Park is the wild, free-flowing, beating heart of the Greater Yellowstone Ecosystem. Its real showstoppers are the geysers and hot springs – nature's crowd-pleasers – but at every turn this land of fire and brimstone breathes, belches and bubbles like a giant kettle on the boil.

Great For...

State
Wyoming

Entrance Fee
7-day pass per vehicle/pedestrian
$35/20

Area
3472 sq miles

Yellowstone is split into five distinct regions – Canyon Country, Geyser Country, Lake Country, Mammoth Country and Tower-Roosevelt Country – each with unique attractions. Upon entering the park you'll be given a basic map and the park newspaper, *Yellowstone Today*, detailing the excellent ranger-led talks and walks (p182; well worth attending). All the visitor centers have information desks staffed by park rangers who can help you tailor a hike to your tastes, from great photo locations to the best chance of spotting a bear.

❶ Old Faithful

Though it's neither the tallest nor even the most predictable geyser in the park, Old Faithful is the poster child for Yellowstone and a consistent crowd-pleaser. Every 90 minutes or so the geyser spouts some 8000 gallons (150 bathtubs) of water up to 180ft in the air. It's worth viewing the eruption from several locations – the

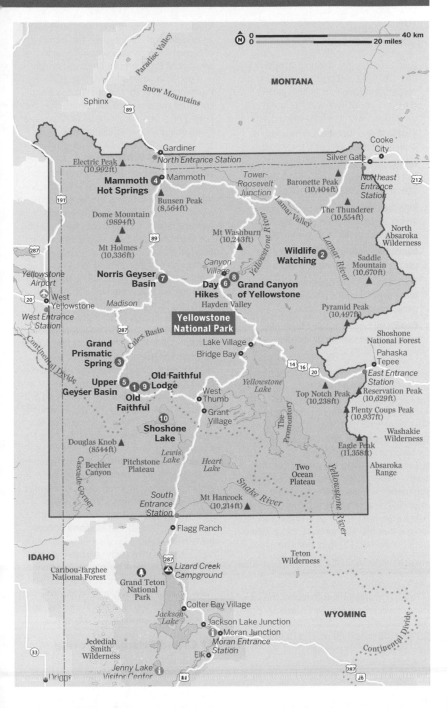

Beating the Crowds

Yellowstone's wonderland attracts up to 30,000 visitors daily in July and August and tops four million gate-crashers annually. Avoid the worst of the crowds with the following advice:

Visit in May or October Services may be limited, but there will be far fewer people.

Hit the trail Most (95%) of visitors never set foot on a backcountry trail; only 1% camp at a backcountry site (permit required).

Bike the park Most campgrounds have underutilized hiker/biker sites, and your skinny tires can slip through any traffic jam.

Mimic the wildlife Be active during the golden hours after dawn and before dusk.

Pack a lunch Eat at one of the park's many overlooked and often lovely scenic picnic areas.

Bundle up Enjoy a private Old Faithful eruption during the winter months.

geyser-side seats, the upper-floor balcony of the **Old Faithful Inn** (☏307-344-7311; www.yellowstonenationalparklodges.com; Old Faithful; Old House d with shared/private bath from $160/260, r $320-390; ☺early May-early Oct) and (highly recommended) from a distance on Observation Hill.

For over 75 years the geyser faithfully erupted every hour or so – one reason for the name the Washburn expedition gave it in 1870. The average time between shows these days is 90 minutes and getting longer, though this has historically varied between 45 and 110 minutes. The average eruption lasts around four minutes. The water temperature is normally 204°F (95°C) and the steam is about 350°F (176°C). The longer the eruption, the longer the recovery time. Rangers correctly predict eruptions to within 10 minutes about 90% of the time. And no, Old Faithful has never erupted on the hour.

A fairly reliable method of calculating exactly when an eruption of Old Faithful is imminent is to count the number of people seated around the geyser – the number of tourists is inversely proportional to the amount of time left until the next eruption.

If you find yourself twiddling your thumbs waiting for the old salt, pause to consider the power of recycling – you are sitting on a boardwalk made from around three million recycled plastic water jugs.

❷ Wildlife Watching

Along with the big mammals – grizzly, black bear, moose and bison – Yellowstone is home to elk, pronghorn antelope and bighorn sheep. Wolves have been part of the national park since reintroduction in 1996. Native to the area, both wolves and bison nearly met extinction because of hunting and human encroachment. While their numbers have resurged, taking them off the endangered species list means they can now be legally hunted outside park boundaries.

In Yellowstone's heart between Yellowstone Lake and Canyon Village, **Hayden Valley** is your best all-round bet for wildlife viewing. For the best chances of seeing wildlife, head out at dawn or dusk and stake out a turnout anywhere off the Grand Loop Rd. Bring patience and binoculars – a grizzly just might wander into your viewfinder, or perhaps you'll spy a rutting elk or hear the bugle of a solitary moose reaching the river for a drink.

Lamar Valley, in the northeast, is where wolves were first reintroduced and is ground zero for spotting them. Ask rangers where packs are most active or attend a wolf-watching (or other) excursion with the recommended **Yellowstone Forever Institute** (☏406-848-2400; www.yellowstone.org). Hearing howls echo across the valley at dusk is a magical, primeval experience. Following flash floods in June 2022, the valley was temporarily closed to visitors, so check with the National Park Service for access information before you set off.

❸ Grand Prismatic Spring

At 370ft wide and 121ft deep, Grand Prismatic Spring is the park's largest and deepest hot spring. It's also considered by many to be the most beautiful thermal feature in the park. Boardwalks lead around the multicolored mist of the gorgeous pool and its spectacularly colored rainbow rings of algae. From above, the spring looks like a giant blue eye weeping exquisite multi-colored tears.

❹ Mammoth Hot Springs

The imposing **Lower** and **Upper Terraces** of Mammoth Hot Springs are the highlight of the Mammoth region. An hour's worth of boardwalks wind their way between ornate and graceful limestone pools, ledges and plateaus. **Palette Springs** (accessed from the lower parking lot) and sulfur-yellow **Canary Springs** (accessed from the upper loop, 1km south) are the most beautiful sites, but thermal activity is constantly in flux, so check the current state of play at the visitor center.

❺ Upper Geyser Basin

While Old Faithful gets the most attention, there's lots to explore in Upper Geyser Basin, which has the densest collection of geysers in Yellowstone. On Geyser Hill you'll find charismatic **Anemone** and fickle **Beehive Geysers**. If you see a group of backpack- and radio-wielding Geyser Gazers huddled near the latter, stick around for an impressive show. Below, fantastic **Castle Geyser** is one of the largest formations of its kind in the world, and the view from **Daisy Geyser** is excellent.

❻ Day Hikes

Even if you drive every road in Yellowstone you'll still see only 2% of the park. Easily the best way to get a close-up taste of Yellowstone's unique combination of rolling landscape, wildlife and thermal activity is on foot, along the 900-plus miles of maintained trails.

Hiking is also the best way to escape the summer crowds. Only 10% of visitors step off the road or boardwalks, only half of those venture further than a mile and just 1% overnight in the backcountry. It's one thing to photograph a bison from your car; it's quite another to hike gingerly past a snorting herd out on their turf. So pick up a map, pack some granola bars and work at least a couple of great hikes into your Yellowstone itinerary.

Grand Prismatic Spring

Where you hike depends on when you visit the park. Early in summer (May, June) you'll likely have to focus on the north of the park around the Mammoth and Tower-Roosevelt regions. Snowfall and bear restrictions close many higher-altitude hikes and regions around Yellowstone Lake until the middle of July. Many hikes in the centre and south of the park are muddy or snowy until July, so bring appropriate footwear.

If you're a novice hiker consider joining a **ranger hike**. These change from year to year, subject to budget and staffing constraints, but at present rangers lead summertime hikes to Mystic Falls, along the south rim of the Canyon region and to Storm Point, as well as several boardwalk strolls at places like Mud Volcano. Check the park newspaper for details.

Note that the park uses a three-character code (eg 2K7) to identify both trailheads and specific backcountry campsites.

❼ Norris Geyser Basin

Norris Geyser Basin comprises **Porcelain Basin** and **Back Basin**, accessed through two connecting loops. If the world's tallest geyser, **Steamboat Geyser**, isn't erupting (it probably isn't), continue around to the explosive remains of **Porkchop Geyser** and the appropriately named **Vixen Geyser**, whose random machine-gun eruptions will beguile you.

❽ Grand Canyon of Yellowstone

Near Canyon Village, this is one of the park's true blockbuster sights. After its placid meanderings north from Yellowstone Lake, the Yellowstone River suddenly plummets over Upper Falls and then the much larger Lower Falls before raging through the 1000ft-deep canyon. Scenic overlooks and a network of trails along the canyon's rims highlight its multicolored beauty from a dozen angles – South Rim Dr leads to the most spectacular overlook, at **Artist Point**.

❾ Old Faithful Inn

Designed by Seattle architect Robert C Reamer and built in 1904, this is the only building in the park that looks as though it actually belongs here. The log rafters of its

Lower Falls

PATRICK ORTON/GETTY IMAGES ©

seven-story lobby rise nearly 80ft, and the chimney of the central fireplace (actually eight fireplaces combined) contains more than 500 tons of rhyolite rock. It's definitely a worthwhile visit, even for nonguests.

The Crow's Nest, a top-floor balcony where musicians once played for dancers in the lobby below, is wonderful (but unused since 1959). Look also for the huge popcorn popper and fire tools at the back of the fireplace. The 2nd-floor **observation deck** offers the chance to enjoy fine views of **Old Faithful geyser** over a drink, and the lobby hosts local artists and authors. Free 45-minute Historic Inn tours depart from the fireplace at 9:30am, 11am, 2pm and 3:30pm.

The inn's biggest secret? If you make a request when you book your room a year in advance, you just might be one of half a dozen people allowed up on the rooftop to watch the flags being lowered at around 6pm. The geyser-basin views are unparalleled.

❿ Shoshone Lake

The largest backcountry lake in the lower 48, Shoshone Lake spells paradise for canoeists and kayakers. The serene lake is closed to motorized vessels and is lined with a dozen secluded boater-only campsites. On its far western edge, Shoshone Geyser Basin's pools, thermals and mud pots make up the largest backcountry thermal area in the park. One-third of all of Yellowstone's backcountry use takes place along its shores, which are accessible only to hikers and hand-propelled boats.

Boaters must access the lake up the channel from Lewis Lake. From mid-July to August the channel requires portage of a few hundred yards in cold water (bring appropriate footwear), though in spring you can often paddle through.

Of 20 lakeshore campsites, 13 are reserved for boaters, four for hikers and three are shared. All have pit toilets. Rangers claim the nicest campsites are 8Q4, 8R4 and 8R1. Wood fires are not allowed along the lakeshore.

🥾 Overnight Hikes

There's no better way to experience the raw wildness of Yellowstone than on an overnight backpacking trip. Some experience of backcountry camping is important before heading out into the wild, particularly in bear awareness, hanging food and leave-no-trace practices. That said, there's a huge range of challenges available, from easy strolls, to easy backcountry overnights an hour from the road, to multiday expedition-style traverses of the Thorofare corner or Gallatin Range through some of the remotest terrain south of Alaska. Choose the right trip at the right time of year and arrive prepared, and there's no better way to experience the park.

If you don't fancy organizing a multiday trek yourself, consider a company like **Trail Guides Yellowstone** (☏406-595-1823; www.trailguides yellowstone.com; 2149 Durston Rd, Unit 35, Bozeman) or **Wildland Trekking Company** (☏800-715-4453; www.wildland trekking.com; 2304 N 7th Ave, Unit K, Bozeman), both based in Bozeman, MT, whose backpacking trips cost $255 to $270 per person per day, including meals, guide and transportation from Bozeman. Wildland Trekking Company even offers llama treks.

Most boaters make their first camp on the southern shore (campsites nearest to the channel are reserved for first- and last-night use only). If you need to cross the lake, do so early in the morning and at the half-mile-wide Narrows in the center of the lake. Prevailing winds are from the southwest and pick up after noon. The lake is icebound until mid-June, when flooding is possible at shoreline campsites. Backcountry boating campsites at Shoshone Lake cannot be reserved before July 1 or 15, depending on the site.

Hike Mt Washburn

MATL TRAIN/SHUTTERSTOCK ©

This popular return hike climbs gradually to the fire lookout tower on the summit of 10,243ft Mt Washburn for some of the park's best views. Over 10,000 hikers tackle this trail annually, so leave early to get trailhead parking. Older teenagers should be able to do the hike.

Mt Washburn is all that remains of a volcano that erupted around 640,000 years ago, forming the vast Yellowstone caldera. Interpretive displays in the lookout tower point out the caldera extents, making this a memorable place to get a sense of the awesome scale of the Yellowstone supervolcano. The peak is named after Montana surveyor-general Henry Washburn, who rode up the peak to see the view during the Washburn, Langford and Doane expedition of 1870.

The route described here starts from Dunraven Pass (8859ft) on the Grand Loop

Duration 4 hours

Distance 6.4 miles round-trip

Difficulty Moderate

Elevation Change 1400ft

Start & Finish Dunraven Pass trailhead

Nearest Town/Junction
Canyon Village

Rd, 4.8 miles north of Canyon and 14.2 miles south of Tower. An alternative route begins from the larger Chittenden parking area (5 miles north of the pass) for a marginally shorter but less interesting hike (but good bike trail) to the summit. Use Trails Illustrated's 1:63,360 map No 304 *Tower/Canyon*.

Snow often obstructs the Dunraven Pass approach through the end of June. Wildflower displays in July and August are legendary. Frequent afternoon thunderstorms

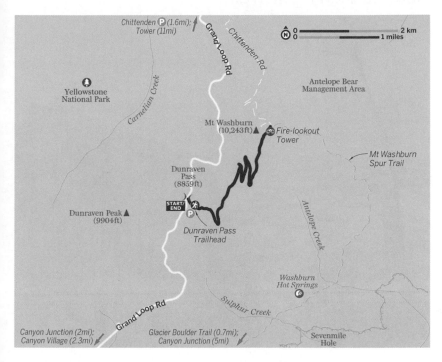

bring fierce winds and lightning, so pack a windbreaker even if the weather looks clear and be ready to make a quick descent if a storm rolls in.

Keep in mind that grizzlies flock to Mt Washburn's eastern slopes in large numbers during August and September in search of ripening whitebark pine nuts.

The wide trail follows a rough, disused road (dating from 1905) and so makes for a comfortable, steady ascent, following a series of long, ribbon-like loops through a forest of subalpine firs. After 20 minutes the views start to open up. The fire tower appears dauntingly distant, but the climb really isn't as painful as it looks. Continue northeast up broad switchbacks to a viewpoint, then follow a narrow ridge past a few stunted whitebark pines (look out for bears) to the gravel **Chittenden Rd** at the Mt Washburn Trail junction. At the junction the road curves up to the three-story

fire-lookout tower, about two hours from the trailhead. The side trail right at the junction leads down the Mt Washburn Spur Trail to Canyon Junction.

The viewing platform and ground-level public observation room has restrooms (but no water), a public 20x Zeiss telescope, displays on the Yellowstone caldera and graphics to help you identify the surrounding peaks and valleys. The fire tower was built in the 1930s and is one of three in the park still staffed from June to October. The majestic panoramas (when the weather is clear) stretch over three-quarters of the park, across the Yellowstone caldera south to Yellowstone Lake, Canyon, the Hayden Valley and even the Tetons, and north to the Beartooth and Absaroka Ranges. Below you are the smoking Washburn Hot Springs. Keep your eyes peeled for bighorn sheep basking near the summit.

Hike Bunsen Peak Trail

TANGENT IMAGEZ/SHUTTERSTOCK ©

Bunsen Peak (8564ft) is a popular half-day hike, and you can extend it to a more demanding day hike by continuing down the mountain's gentler eastern slope to the Bunsen Peak Rd and then waaay down (800ft) to the base of seldom-visited Osprey Falls.

The initial Bunsen Peak Trail climbs east out of Gardner's Hole to the exposed summit of Bunsen Peak, offering outstanding panoramas of Mammoth, the Gallatin Range, Swan Lake Flat and the Blacktail Deer Plateau. Even if you just make it halfway up the hill you'll be rewarded with superb views.

Bunsen Peak was named by the 1872 Hayden Survey for German scientist Robert Wilhelm Eberhard von Bunsen (after whom the Bunsen burner was also named), whose pioneering theories about the inner workings of Icelandic geysers influenced early Yellowstone hydrothermal research. The mountain is actually an ancient lava plug,

Duration 2½ hours

Distance 4.2-mile round-trip

Difficulty Moderate

Elevation Change 1300ft

Start & Finish Bunsen Peak trailhead

Nearest Town/Junction Mammoth

the surrounding volcanic walls of which have partly eroded away. So, yes, you are climbing the inside of a former volcano!

From the Mammoth Visitor Center, drive 4.5 miles south on Grand Loop Rd, cross the light-colored rock defile of the **Golden Gate** and turn left into the unpaved parking area on the eastern side of the road, just beyond the Rustic Falls turnout. The parking lot is small and fills up quickly, so either get here early, try the Glen Creek trailhead across the road or continue a little further to Swan Lake Flat.

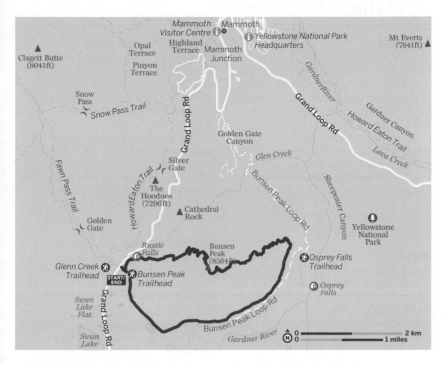

From 7250ft, the well-trodden single-track dirt trail branches left just beyond a barricade on the left (north) side of unpaved **Bunsen Peak Rd**. The trail climbs immediately through sagebrush interspersed with wildflowers, then enters a young Douglas fir and lodgepole pine mosaic. You'll get early views of the Golden Gate pass below and to the left, and the ash-colored jumble of the limestone Hoodoos to the north. About half an hour from the trailhead a series of meadows offers fabulous views southwest to Swan Lake Flat, Antler Peak (10,023ft), Mt Holmes (10,336ft), Terraced Mountain and Electric Peak (10,992ft).

Five minutes later, at one of the many switchbacks, you'll gain a great view of the eroded sandstone cliffs and spires of **Cathedral Rock**, with vistas down to the red roofs and bleached travertine mounds of Mammoth. The layered sandstone-and-shale mountain of Mt Everts (7841ft), to

the north, offers proof that the area was underwater 70 to 140 million years ago.

Beyond the Cathedral Rock outcrop, the switchbacks get steeper on the north side of the mountain and the exposed dome-shaped peak comes into view. Keep your eyes peeled for bighorn sheep.

The trail passes under electricity wires before a small cabin and communications equipment marks the first of three small summits, 2.1 miles from the trailhead. Continue east along the loose talus ridge, past the cairns of the middle summit, to the exposed easternmost summit for the best southern panoramas. Electric Peak, one of the highest in the Gallatin Range, looms largest to the northwest, marking the park's northern boundary, with the Absaroka Range to the northeast.

Either retrace your steps down the western slope or wind around the peak to descend the unsigned eastern slope to the Osprey Falls Trail.

Essential Information

Sleeping

Although competition for campsites and lodging may be fierce, there's nothing quite like falling asleep to the eerie sounds of bugling elk and howling wolves and waking to the sulfur smell of the earth erupting and bubbling.

You can make reservations for park accommodations and five of the park's 12 campgrounds through the park concessionaire **Yellowstone National Park Lodges** (Xanterra; ☑307-344-7311, 866-439-7375; www.yellowstonenationalparklodges.com). Online bookings are essential for both hotels and campgrounds.

Eating

Food in the park is split between campfire cuisine, cafeteria food, a couple of fast-food choices and the more pleasant dining rooms of the park's historic inns. Yellowstone National Park Lodges runs most dining options, so don't be surprised if you get a serious dose of déjà vu every time you open a menu. That said, most places are pretty good value considering the prime real estate and there have been significant moves in recent years to add a range of healthy, gluten-free and locally sourced options. You can preview park menus at www.yellowstonenationalparklodges.com.

The park's cafeterias are bland but convenient, and reasonably economical for families. All places serve breakfast and most offer an all-you-can-eat buffet that can quickly wipe out even the best-laid hiking plans. Kids' menus are available almost everywhere. Almost all offer sandwiches for lunch and heavier, pricier and more interesting fare for dinner.

There's also fast food at major junctions, plus snack shops and grocery supplies in the Yellowstone General Stores. The Grant Village, Old Faithful Inn and Lake Yellowstone Hotel dining rooms all require dinner reservations.

Getting There & Away

Most visitors to Yellowstone fly into Jackson, WY, or Bozeman, MT, but it's often more affordable to choose Billings, MT. You will need a car; there is no public transportation to or within Yellowstone National Park.

The closest airport to the park is **Yellowstone Airport** (WYS; ☑406-646-7631; www.yellowstoneairport.org; ⊘late May-Sep), in West Yellowstone, MT. It has three daily summer flights (end May through September) to and from Salt Lake City, UT, with SkyWest/Delta. Closes in winter.

Getting Around

Unless you're part of a guided bus tour, the only way to get around is to drive. There is no public transportation within the park, except for a few ski-drop services during winter.

Yellowstone Roadrunner (☑406-640-0631; www.yellowstoneroadrunner.com) Taxi and charter service in West Yellowstone that offers one-way drops and shuttles for backpacking trips, though it's not cheap.

Park Entrances

Park entrances are open to vehicles 24 hours a day during open months. The **North Entrance** is at Gardiner, MT, and the **Northeast Entranc**e is near Cooke City; both are open year-round. The **East Entrance** is on US 14/16/20, from Cody, WY, and the **South Entrance** is on US 89/191/287, north of Grand Teton National Park; both are open early May to early November. The **West Entrance** is on US 20/191/287 near West Yellowstone, MT, and is open mid- or late April to early November. ∎

Old Faithful

Yellowstone's Thermal Features

Fueled by its underground furnace, Yellowstone is a bubbling cauldron of more than 10,000 geothermal features – more than all other geothermal areas on the planet combined. The average heat flow from the region is 40 times the global average.

Geysers

Only a handful of Yellowstone's thermal features are active geysers (from the Icelandic *geysir,* meaning 'to gush or rage'), but these still comprise about 50% of the global total, making the park a globally significant resource.

Yellowstone Lake

One of the world's largest alpine lakes, Yellowstone Lake was formed by the collapse of the Yellowstone caldera and shaped by glacial erosion. Hydrothermal explosions have further shaped the shoreline.

Travertine Terraces

The limestone rock of the Mammoth region contrasts with the silica-rich rhyolite found elsewhere in the park. Here, carbon dioxide in the hot water forms carbonic acid, which then dissolves the surrounding limestone (calcium carbonate). As this watery solution breaks the surface, some carbon dioxide escapes from the solution and limestone is deposited as travertine, forming beautiful terraces.

Mud Pots

Are Yellowstone's mud pots really boiling? No, the bubbling is actually the release of steam and gas. Sulfur and iron content give rise to the nickname 'paint pots.'

Fumaroles

Essentially dry geysers, fumaroles' water boils away before reaching the surface, where they burst with heat. These steam vents also give off carbon dioxide and some hydrogen sulfide (that nice 'rotten egg' smell) with a hiss or roaring sound.

Grand Prismatic Spring, Yellowstone National Park (p180)

In Focus

Grizzly bear, Yellowstone National Park (p178)

FRANK FICHTMUELLER/SHUTTERSTOCK ©

The Parks Today

Following a 2016 anniversary that celebrated a century in which the US National Park Service grew from 12 parks to 60, 2017 brought new challenges to America's protected areas. The Trump administration's downsizing of several national monuments left many reflecting on the precarious nature of America's great natural landscapes and our unending duty to protect them for future generations. While some of those measures were overturned by President Biden, the future remains anything but secure.

Trump, Bears Ears & Beyond

The Trump administration was unconventional in many ways, but it sent an existential shiver down the spines of conservationists everywhere when it took aim at Utah's Bears Ears National Monument, which protected land sacred to the Pueblo peoples, the Navajo and the Ute. Bears Ears shrank by around 85%, from 1.35 million acres to 160,000 acres, and 1996-designated Grand Staircase–Escalante National Monument, also in Utah, was almost halved in size. The move was unprecedented. While presidents have shrunk national monuments in the past, most recently in the early 1960s, it has never been undertaken on such a significant scale. President Biden would later reverse the decision on coming to office in 2021, but the whole episode cast hitherto unforeseen doubt on how enduring national park protections might be.

Funding the NPS

Despite record-breaking park visitor numbers in 2016, the 2018 federal budget contained cuts of around $300 million to the NPS's operating budget, prompting the NPS to warn of possible staff cuts, campground closures, reduced operating hours and otherwise reduced services in up to 90% of its parks. After winning the 2020 election, President Biden restored much of the NPS's budget funding. In 2022, the Biden administration announced a 2023 budget of $3.6 billion dollars for the National Park Service, an increase of $492.2 million when compared with the previous year; the 2020 budget was $2.7 billion.

Climate Change

Climate change is another existential threat to the national parks in both the near and long-term future, whether it be in the form of more intense and frequent wildfires in the West or devastating hurricanes in the southeast. The most obvious consequences can already be seen in Glacier National Park, where rapidly melting glaciers may render a name-change by 2030.

To complicate matters further, in 2022 a conservative majority on the US Supreme Court ruled against the Environmental Protection Agency (EPA) and severely restricted its ability to limit carbon and other emissions from the fossil-fuel industry. Seen as a major blow to any attempts by the federal government to tackle climate change, the court's ruling could have devastating impacts upon the health of the nation's ecosystems and its national parks.

The Wolf Question

From a conservation perspective, the return of gray wolves to Yellowstone in 1995 has been an unqualified success (p209). From 41 wolves reintroduced into the park in 1995, the park's population has grown to nearly 100, with around 500 across the Greater Yellowstone area. The population has even dispersed as far away as California.

But not everyone has been as thrilled with the rise in wolf numbers. Ranchers and hunters across Wyoming, Montana, Idaho and elsewhere have declared open season on wolves. In late 2020, President Trump obliged, removing all federal endangered species protections for wolves, which conservationists warned was premature.

In the last six months of 2021 alone, 20 of Yellowstone's wolves that strayed beyond the park boundaries were shot, effectively wiping out the Phantom Lake pack. Even Montana's governor Greg Gianforte had trapped and killed a collared Yellowstone wolf earlier in 2021.

Wolves will probably survive the conservative backlash against the wolf's return, at least inside the park. But their role in America's wild spaces remains one of the hottest topics in the West.

SHAWN WALTERS/EYEEM/GETTY IMAGES ©

History

Few things are as quintessentially American as national parks. Their genesis, implementation and growth since 1872 is a work of genius second only to the US Constitution. A handful of people once had the foresight to pull the reins in on rampant hunting, logging, mining and tourist development, so that we might save at least some of our most magnificent treasures for future generations – their actions constitute one of the greatest chapters in US history.

1864
President Lincoln designates Yosemite Valley and the Mariposa Grove a protected state park.

1872
President Ulysses S Grant designates Yellowstone the world's first national park.

1890
Yosemite National Park is established, but the state of California retains control of Yosemite Valley and Mariposa Grove.

Bison, Yellowstone National Park (p178)

A Magnificent Park

American portrait artist George Catlin (1796–1872) is credited with being the first person to conceptualize a 'nation's park.' He envisioned a 'magnificent park' to protect the country's remaining indigenous people, buffalo and wilderness from the onslaught of western expansion. But more than three decades would pass before anything remotely resembling that vision existed.

In 1851, members of an armed militia accidentally rode into a massive granite valley in the Sierra Nevada and decided to call it 'Yosemity,' possibly a corruption of the Miwok word *Oo-hoo'-ma-te* or *uzumatel*, meaning 'grizzly bear.' The name stuck, and soon word of the valley and its waterfalls got out. Within no time, entrepreneurs were divvying up the land in hopes of profiting from tourists.

Thanks to a handful of outspoken writers, artists and naturalists, and – most importantly – the efforts of the great landscape architect Frederick Law Olmsted, Yosemite Valley was spared privatization. In 1864 President Abraham Lincoln signed a bill into law that put

1894
After a poacher is caught killing bison in Yellowstone, Congress grants the park the power to enforce conservation laws.

1916
Stephen Mather convinces the Dept of the Interior to create the National Park Service.

1923
Yosemite's Hetch Hetchy Valley is dammed, the first shot in a continuing battle between conservationists and developers.

The Father of Our National Parks

Often considered the 'father of the US national park system,' Scottish-born John Muir (1838–1914) was an eloquent writer, naturalist and arguably the greatest defender of wilderness areas in the late 19th century. It should be noted, however, that he has recently become a more controversial figure as people have become increasingly aware of his racist views on Native Americans and African Americans.

Nonetheless, his writings were pivotal in the creation not just of Yosemite, but of Sequoia, Mt Rainier, Petrified Forest and Grand Canyon National Parks. Famously – but unsuccessfully – Muir fought to save Yosemite's Hetch Hetchy Valley, which he believed rivaled Yosemite Valley in beauty and grandeur. Although he couldn't stop the damming of the river, his writings on the issue cemented the now widely held belief that our national parks should remain as close as possible to their natural state.

Yosemite Valley, and the nearby Mariposa Grove of giant sequoias, under the control of California. Although it wasn't a national park, it was the first time *any* government had mandated the protection of a natural area for public use.

Birth of a National Park

Four years later, a group of men bankrolled by Northern Pacific Railroad headed into the Wyoming wilderness to investigate reports of thermal pools and geysers. Among their discoveries were the Great Fountain Geyser and another geyser they would name Old Faithful. Soon, lobbyists at Northern Pacific, with their eyes on tourist dollars, rallied alongside conservationists for a public park like Yosemite. In 1872 Ulysses S Grant signed the landmark Yellowstone National Park Act, creating the country's first national park.

Meanwhile, in Yosemite, the famed naturalist John Muir lamented the destruction that logging companies, miners and sheep – which he famously deemed 'hoofed locusts' – were wreaking upon the park. In 1890 Yosemite became the country's second national park, but it wasn't until 1905 that Muir convinced Congress to expand the boundaries to include all of Yosemite Valley and the Mariposa Grove.

Over the next 25 years, presidents signed off on six more national parks, including Mt Rainier (1899), Crater Lake (1902) and Glacier (1910).

In 1908 Theodore Roosevelt declared the Grand Canyon a national monument. The act was met with utter outrage from Arizona politicians, mining claim holders and ranchers, who believed he has overstepped his bounds as president – a theme that continues to this day concerning the designation of federal lands.

1926
Yellowstone's last wolves are killed in the federal predator control program, which also targeted mountain lions, bears and coyotes.

1933
FDR creates the Civilian Conservation Corps; CCC workers improve infrastructure in national parks and plant over three billion trees.

1941–49
Ansel Adams photographs every national park in the US, bar the Everglades, for the NPS.

Mather & the National Park Service

Still, there existed no effective protection or management of the new parks until the creation of the National Park Service (NPS) in 1916. The NPS was the brainchild of an industrialist and conservationist named Stephen Mather, who convinced the Dept of the Interior that a single governing body was precisely what the parks needed. When President Woodrow Wilson signed the National Park Service Act into law, Mather became the first director.

Mather believed that the best way to promote and improve the parks was to get people into them. A public relations guru, Mather encouraged park superintendents to run publicity campaigns, created the park ranger system, initiated campfire talks and opened the first park museums. His efforts – always coupled with media outreach – were so successful that by 1928 he had tripled the number of park visitors to three million.

While Mather was extremely successful in developing the parks, some felt he'd gone too far. Conservation groups such as the National Parks Association and the Sierra Club felt that Mather's emphasis on development came at the expense of the parks themselves. Mather's successor and protégé, Horace Albright, partially addressed these concerns by creating a national wildlife division within the NPS.

Theodore Roosevelt: the Conservation President

In 1903, President Theodore Roosevelt undertook a two-month-long campaign tour. In between giving 263 speeches in 25 states, he still managed to spend two weeks exploring Yellowstone and three nights camping out with John Muir in Yosemite. But the greatest legacy of that trip arose from time spent at the Grand Canyon. Upon seeing the canyon for the first time, Roosevelt famously opined that the mystical natural wonder could not be improved by any human intervention – it should be left exactly as it was. A nascent conservationist movement had just gained an influential new member.

Muir may have provided the philosophical underpinnings of the national parks, but it was Roosevelt who transformed the vision into reality. An avid hunter, birder, far-sighted thinker and lover of the outdoors, Roosevelt's time out West – before he became president – profoundly shaped his life and legacy. By the time he left office in 1909, he had signed off on five national parks, 18 national monuments, 51 federal bird sanctuaries and 100 million acres of national forest.

FDR & the CCC

With the Great Depression, the parks went through significant changes. President Franklin Delano Roosevelt created the Civilian Conservation Corps (CCC) and put thousands of young men to work improving national park roads, visitors' shelters, campsites and

1956–66
Mission 66 improves park facilities and creates the first national park visitor centers.

1980
The Alaska National Interest Lands Conservation Act doubles amount of land under control of the NPS.

1995
Forty-one gray wolves are reintroduced to Yellowstone nearly 70 years after they disappeared from the park ecosystem

The Antiquities Act, National Monuments & Other NPS Sites

In 1906 Congress passed the Antiquities Act, which gives the president the authority to protect public land by designating it a national monument. The Act was originally designed to protect Native American archaeological sites out West, and Theodore Roosevelt quickly realized that he could use it to protect any tract of land for any reason – and without opposition from lobbyists or political opponents in Congress. The Grand Canyon was the most famous example of Roosevelt's decisive stroke.

In 2015 there were 117 national monuments, which rose to 129 by 2022. More are designated every year, while others change status. Most are administered by the NPS. Other sites that come under NPS jurisdiction include historic sites and parks, memorials, parkways, seashores, recreation areas and preserves, which are like parks, except that fossil fuel extraction and sport hunting are permitted (many Alaskan parks hold a dual park–preserve status). In total the NPS currently administers over 400 natural and historic sites, including 63 national parks.

trails. During his presidency, FDR also created Joshua Tree, Capitol Reef and Channel Islands National Monuments (all of which would become national parks), and Olympic and Kings Canyon National Parks.

With the beginning of WWII, the country's greatest public relief program came to an end, CCC workers went off to war, and the national park budget was slashed. Simultaneously, postwar prosperity allowed more Americans to travel – and hordes of them headed to the parks. By 1950 some 32 million people had visited America's national parks. Within five years the number topped 60 million.

Mission 66

The number of travelers descending on the parks put tremendous pressure on them. In 1956 NPS Director Conrad Wirth created Mission 66, a 10-year plan to improve park infrastructure and dramatically increase visitors' services. The plan established the first park visitor centers, hired more staff and improved facilities. Over the course of Mission 66, Congress also added more than 50 new protected areas to the national park system.

In 1964 George Hartzog succeeded Wirth as director of the NPS and continued to add new acquisitions. During his tenure, nearly 70 new parks would come under the jurisdiction of the NPS. In 1972 President Nixon replaced Hartzog with his own appointee, and expansions to the park service were halted.

Doubling Down

Little was added to the national parks system until 1980, when President Carter signed the Alaska National Interest Lands Conservation Act into law. The

2011	2013	2014
A proposed ban on the sale of plastic bottles in the Grand Canyon is blocked after Coca-Cola, an NPS donor, expresses displeasure.	Congressional gridlock shuts down the federal government; all national parks are forced to close for a 16-day period.	Park visitation reaches an all-time high with 292.8 million visitors over the course of the year.

landmark legislation instantly protected over 80 million acres and doubled the amount of land under control of the national parks. Ten new national parks and monuments were created in the process. Although controversial in Alaska, the move has been widely heralded as one of the greatest conservation measures in US history.

NPS Logo

The National Park Service adopted its official logo in 1951. Shaped like an arrowhead, it features a bison and sequoia tree set against a snow-capped peak in the background.

The Parks Today

Since Yellowstone was created in 1872, the national park system has grown to encompass over 400 sites and more than 84 million acres. The parks today protect many of the continent's most sensitive ecosystems, some of the world's most remarkable landscapes, and America's most important historical and cultural landmarks. According to the National Park Service, the total number of visitors to US national parks from 1904 to 2021 was nearly 15.4 billion. They are the country's greatest natural treasure.

Despite a steady increase in visitation, however, the parks still face a variety of threats and obstacles, including loss of biodiversity, declining air and water quality, climate disruption and insufficient funding. In 2011, the NPS released a Call to Action: an initiative to help the service prepare for its second century, with aims such as reducing greenhouse gas emissions by 20%, increasing community involvement and continuing to raise awareness for the parks among all Americans.

Hot Topics

While conservationists, policy makers and the NPS debate how to best protect the parks, nearly everyone agrees the parks need money – except, it seems, for Congress. With budget cuts and obstructionist gridlock becoming increasingly the norm in Washington, the NPS has begun to turn to private donors and corporate sponsorships in order to make up for the federal shortfall.

System-wide challenges are not the only matters garnering national attention. Congestion, crowds and cars remain a constant source of concern, and more and more parks are introducing free shuttles to combat traffic and reduce air pollution. And from the ongoing debate about snowmobiles in Yellowstone to the concern about melting glaciers in Glacier National Park, there are plenty of other park-specific issues fueling debate.

2016
The National Park System celebrates the 100th anniversary of its founding.

2019
White Sands in New Mexico becomes the 62nd national park. A year later, New River Gorge in West Virginia becomes the 63rd.

2021
During the COVID-19 pandemic, visitor numbers to parks fall to 237 million. Numbers rebound to 297.1 million in 2021.

MARGARET.WIKTOR/SHUTTERSTOCK ©

Outdoor Activities

We've yet to meet someone visiting a national park so they can hang around inside. The outdoors is what the parks are all about, and getting out usually means getting active. With environments ranging from the Rocky Mountains to the rain-forest-clad Pacific Northwest, the possibilities might just be endless.

Hiking

Nothing encapsulates the spirit of the national parks like hiking. Thousands of miles of trails crisscross the parks, offering access to their most scenic mountain passes, highest waterfalls, deepest canyons and quietest corners. Trails run the gamut of accessibility, from short hikes to a local viewpoint to the thrilling exposed ascent of **Longs Peak** in Rocky Mountain.

Regardless of the style of the trail, you'll find that exploring on foot generally offers the best park experience. The relatively slow pace of walking brings you into closer contact with the wildlife, and allows you to appreciate the way different perspectives and the day's shifting light can alter the scenery. The satisfaction gained from completing a hike is also a

Mt Washburn Trail, Yellowstone National Park (p184)

★ **Classic Day Hikes**

Iceberg Lake (Glacier)

Hoh River Trail (Olympic)

Sky Pond (Rocky Mountain)

Mt Washburn Trail (Yellowstone)

Cascade Pass (North Cascades)

worthy reward; it's one thing to look over the rim of the Black Canyon of the Gunnison, it's another to work up a sweat hiking back up from the canyon floor.

Each park chapter in this guide has its own Hiking or Activities section with descriptions of the parks' top hikes. We've done our best to cover a variety of trails, not just our favorites. Our goal with descriptions is less about navigation than it is about helping you choose which hikes to squeeze into your trip. Detailed trail descriptions and maps are readily available at visitor centers in every park, and they will complement this guide well. Know your limitations, know the route you plan to take and pace yourself.

Backpacking

There are hundreds of amazing day hikes to choose from in the park system, but if you want the full experience, head out into the wilderness on an overnight trip. The claim that 99% of park visitors never make it into the backcountry may not be true everywhere, but you will unquestionably see far fewer people and witness exponentially more magic the further from a road you go. Backcountry campsites are also much more likely to have openings than park lodges and car campsites (which fill up months in advance), making accommodations less of a headache.

Even if you have no backpacking experience, don't consider it out of reach. Most national parks have at least a few backcountry campsites within a couple of hours' walk of a trailhead, making them excellent options for first-time backpackers. You will need gear, however: an appropriate backpack, tent, sleeping bag and pad, stove, headlamp and food are all essential.

Familiarize yourself with the park rules and backcountry ethics before heading out. You will need a permit; if you have your heart set on a famous excursion, apply well in advance online. Most park visitor centers have a backcountry desk, where you can apply for walk-in permits, get trail information, learn about wildlife (bear canisters are generally required in bear country) and check conditions. Before hitting the trail, learn about low-impact camping principles at Leave No Trace (www.lnt.org).

Preparation & Safety

Walks can be as short or long as you like, but remember this when planning: be prepared. The wilderness may be unlike anything you have ever experienced, and designating certain parcels as 'national parks' has not tamed it.

The weather out West can be extraordinary in its unpredictability and sheer force. The summer sun is blazing hot, sudden thunderstorms can drop enough water in 10 minutes to create deadly flash floods, snow can fall at any time of year above the tree line, while ferocious wind storms can rip or blow away your poorly staked tent.

Teton Crest Trail, Grand Teton National Park (p162)

AARON J9/SHUTTERSTOCK ©

★ **Classic Backcountry Trips**

Teton Crest Trail (Grand Teton)

Bechler River (Yellowstone)

Great Northern Traverse (Glacier)

Enchanted Valley Trail (Olympic)

Pacific Coastal Hike (Olympic)

No matter where you are, water should be the number one item on your packing checklist – always carry more than you think you'll need. If you're doing any backpacking, make sure you have a way to purify water, and check with rangers ahead of time about the availability of water along the trail.

If your trip involves any elevation change, take the time to acclimatize before tackling a long hike, to avoid altitude sickness. Sunblock, a hat, ibuprofen and warm wind- and water-proof layers are all non-negotiable at high altitudes. Snow cover can last through the end of June above 11,000ft; check with rangers to see if you'll need gaiters and snowshoes.

After the elements, getting lost is the next major concern. Most day hikes are well signed and visitors are numerous, but you should always take some sort of map. If you plan on going into the backcountry, definitely take a topographic (topo) map and a compass. You can pick up detailed maps in most visitor centers; National Geographic's *Trails Illustrated* series is generally excellent.

At lower elevations and in desert parks, always inquire about ticks, poison oak, poison ivy and rattlesnakes before heading out. Most day hikes are on well-maintained trails, but it's good to know what's out there.

And all hikers, solo or not, should always remember the golden rule: let someone know where you are going and how long you plan to be gone.

Rafting, Kayaking & Canoeing

Rafts, kayaks, canoes and larger boats are a wonderful way to get to parts of the parks that landlubbers can't reach. River-running opportunities abound in the parks. The **Snake River** in Grand Teton National Park has rafting for all skill levels. For a family-friendly trip, there's inner tubing along the **Medano Creek** past the sand dunes in Colorado's Great Sand Dunes National Park.

In Glacier National Park, the lake paddling is excellent and accessible, thanks to boat ramps and rentals on several lakes. In Grand Teton, **String** and **Leigh Lakes** are great for family and novice paddlers, and you can rent boats at Colter Bay. Yellowstone's **Shoshone Lake** is the largest backcountry lake in the lower 48, and offers boat-in access to some of the remotest areas of the park.

Up in the Pacific Northwest, the **Upper Skagit** in North Cascades is excellent for family-friendly Class II or III rafting. **Diablo Lake** in North Cascades and **Lake Crescent** in Olympic National Park are popular spots for kayaking and canoeing.

Rock Climbing & Mountaineering

There's no sport quite like rock climbing. From a distance it appears to be a feat of sheer strength, but balance, creativity, technical know-how and a Zen-like sang-froid are all parts of the game.

Closely related to rock climbing is mountaineering: the technical ascent of a summit, involving ropes, climbing equipment, and, when there are glaciers, ice axes and crampons.

Long-Distance Trails

The 2663-mile **Pacific Crest Trail**, which extends from Canada to Mexico, passes through seven national parks. Similar in nature, the **Continental Divide Trail** (3100 miles) follows the Rockies, passing through Rocky Mountain, Yellowstone and Glacier National Parks.

The Cascade volcanoes and jutting spires in Oregon and Washington present climbers with ample choices, from easier day-long up-and-backs to multiday technical challenges. Highlights include **Mt Rainier** and **North Cascades**. Inexperienced climbers should seek out guide services, as bagging these peaks can be a hazardous proposition. Professional guide companies include American Alpine Institute (www.alpineinstitute.com) in Washington and Timberline Mountain Guides (www.timberlinemtguides.com) in Oregon. Oregon's Mazamas (www.mazamas.org) is a nonprofit mountaineering organization that offers hikes and climbs for both members and nonmembers.

Mountaineering routes are a dime a dozen out West; some of the most famous summits include **Longs Peak** (Rocky Mountain) and **Grand Teton**. Another incredible locale to rope up includes the awe-inspiring peaks of **Glacier National Park**. Because of the exposure and high altitude on these routes, the risks can be high. Like rock climbing, you'll want to hire a guide if you don't already have significant experience.

Cycling & Mountain Biking

As a general rule, expect more options for two-wheeled fun just outside park boundaries. A cyclist could hardly ask for more than the Pacific Northwest has to offer. Beyond the bike-friendly urban centers, there are diverse and spectacular cycling opportunities on the coast, in high deserts, through lush rain forest and up alpine mountains. Many ski resorts turn into mountain-biking destinations in summer. Local shops are great resources for route and back-road suggestions, and visitor centers will have local route maps.

For a challenge, cycle the scenic loop around **Mt Rainier**. Near Mt St Helens, the Plains of Abraham/Ape Canyon Trail and the Lewis River Trail provide top-notch mountain biking in staggering Cascade scenery. Around the Cascade Range there are magnificent cycling destinations: the Cascade Lakes Hwy (Hwy 46) is stunningly beautiful, as is the Diamond Lake to Crater Lake challenge.

For an even greater challenge, try the rough trails of **Great Sand Dunes** in Colorado.

Winter Sports

Cross-Country Skiing & Snowshoeing

Come winter, trails and roads in many parks get blanketed with snow and the crowds disappear. It's a magical time to visit, and those willing to step into skis or snowshoes and brave the elements will be rewarded. The best parks for both activities are Glacier,

★ **So Much to Do...**

For those that want to try it all, here's some more fodder for fun:

Soaking Submerge your sore muscles in thermal hot springs at Yellowstone, Olympic or Crater Lake.

Glissading Take your ice axe and slide down the snow fields on Mt Rainier.

Tide pooling Olympic is tide-pool heaven.

Sand surfing Rent a board, a sled or simply slide on your butt in Colorado's Great Sand Dunes.

Caving Disappear underground into Boulder Cave at Mt Rainier.

Olympic National Park (p122)

ZACH HOLMES/ALAMY STOCK PHOTO ©

Yellowstone, Grand Teton, Rocky Mountain, Olympic, Crater Lake and Mt Rainier, though this is far from a comprehensive list.

In most of these parks, rangers lead snowshoe hikes, which can be an excellent entry to the sport and a great way to learn about the winter environment. Visitor centers are the best place to check for information.

Downhill Skiing & Snowboarding

Most of the best downhill skiing takes place outside the parks. One park, however, does have downhill ski resorts: **Hurricane Ridge**, just inside the border of Olympic National Park, has only three lifts and is the westernmost ski resort in the lower 48. The most notable skiing adjacent to parks covered in this guide is **Jackson Hole**, Wyoming, which has long runs, deep powder and a screeching 4139ft vertical drop.

Swimming

With the exception of the higher-elevation parks (like Glacier and Rocky Mountain), summer means heat, and heat means swimming. Alpine lakes make for wonderful but often frigid swimming, and many of the larger lakes have beaches and designated swimming areas.

As river rats the world over will attest, nothing beats dipping into a swimming hole and drip-drying on a rock in the sun. But be careful – every year, swimmers drown in national park rivers. Always check with visitor centers about trouble spots and the safest places to swim. Unless you're certain about the currents, swim only where others are swimming.

Top places to get wet are **Sedge Bay** in Yellowstone, **Leigh Lake** in Grand Teton, and **Sol Duc Hot Springs** or **Lake Quinault** in Olympic.

Fishing

For many, the idea of heading to the national parks without a fishing rod is ludicrous. Yellowstone offers some of the best fly-fishing in the country. Olympic's **Hoh** and **Sol Duc Rivers** are famous for their runs of salmon and winter steelhead, while the trout fishing is good at the park's **Lake Crescent**. **Glacier** and **Grand Teton** offer outstanding fishing, while fisherfolk flock to **Black Canyon of the Gunnison** for the trout (not to mention the dramatic backdrop).

Wherever you fish, read up on local regulations. Fishing permits are always required, and those caught fishing without one will be fined. (Children under 15 are generally not required to have a license.) Some waters, including many streams and rivers, are catch-and-release only, and sometimes bait-fishing is prohibited. Certain native fish, such as bull trout, kokanee salmon and wild steelhead, are often protected, and anglers in possession of these can be heavily fined. The best place to check regulations is online. For details on regulations, check the park's NPS website (www.nps.gov) and refer to the respective state's department of fish and game website. Find the latter by searching for the state plus 'fish and game.'

Horseback & Mule Riding

Our most time-tested form of transport still makes for a wonderful way to experience the great outdoors. Horseback riding is possible in many of the parks, and outfitters within or immediately outside the parks offer everything from two-hour rides to full- and multiday pack trips. Rides run around $40 per hour or $80 per half-day.

Moose, Grand Teton National Park (p152)

CHASE DEKKER WILD-LIFE IMAGES/GETTY IMAGES ©

Wildlife Watching

It's no coincidence that the establishment of many of the earliest national parks coincided with the first wave of near mass extinctions in the United States: by the 1890s the passenger pigeon, bison, eastern elk, wolf, mountain lion and grizzly bear – along with their habitats and numerous less-heralded species – were all on the verge of disappearing forever. Today, some of these animals have made a comeback, thanks in large part to the protection afforded by the national parks.

Bison

The American bison (or Great American buffalo) is the USA's national animal and the symbol of the devastation wrought upon the wildlife of the American West, but also its part renewal. Ten thousand years ago, vast herds of bison wandered from Alaska to New Mexico and all the way east to Florida. They play an important role in the mythology of many Native American tribes, who hunted the bison for meat and skins. The estimated population at the end of the 18th century was around 65 million – in herds so thick they 'darkened the whole plains,' as explorers Lewis and Clark wrote. By 1889, there were just 541 bison left in America.

What could have been a disaster instead became a turning point. Thanks to the determined intervention of George Bird Grinnell, editor of *Forest and Stream* and founder of the Audubon Society, and a young politician by the name of Theodore Roosevelt, Congress passed an 1894 law granting national parks the power to protect all wildlife within their boundaries. Previous to this, poachers were simply expelled from park lands; now they could be arrested.

Overcoming near extinction, new herds arose from the last survivors, so that one of America's noblest animals can again be admired in its gruff majesty. These days, there are believed to be somewhere between 15,000 and 30,000 bison roaming free, with a total population of half a million on fenced and private lands. The easiest places to see them are Yellowstone National Park and Grand Teton National Park and surrounds in Wyoming.

In winter, the bison sports a long shaggy brown coat, which becomes a lighter brown and lighter-weight in summer; calves are a much lighter shade of brown. Up to 9.2ft long and weighing 2800lb, bisons are herbivores that graze on grasslands – the prairie is their natural habitat – usually in the same area for a couple of hours before moving on; they are known to move up to 2 miles in a day. They can be very fast, running at up to 40mph; in the last two decades of the 20th century, bisons injured more people in Yellowstone National Park (79) than did bears (24).

Moose & Other Grazers

Other large grazers are commonplace throughout many parks. Moose, the largest of the world's deer species, stand 5ft to 7ft at the shoulder and can weigh up to 1000lb. They're common in Yellowstone, Glacier, Rocky Mountain and Grand Teton. The same parks are home to elk, which grow antlers up to 5ft long and weigh up to 700lb. These

Return of the Wolf

The wolf is a potent symbol of America's wilderness. This smart, social predator is the largest species of canine – averaging more than 100lb and reaching nearly 3ft at the shoulder. An estimated 400,000 once roamed the continent.

Wolves were not regarded warmly by European settlers. The first wildlife legislation in the British colonies was a wolf bounty. And as 19th-century Americans moved west, they replaced the native herds with domestic cattle and sheep, which wolves found equally tasty.

To stop wolves from devouring the livestock, extermination soon became official government policy. Up until 1965, for $20 to $50 an animal, wolves were shot, poisoned, trapped and dragged from dens, until in the lower 48 states only a few hundred gray wolves remained.

In 1944 naturalist Aldo Leopold called for the return of the wolf. His argument was ecology, not nostalgia. Wild ecosystems need their top predators to maintain healthy biodiversity; all animals and plants suffered with the wolf gone.

Protected and encouraged, wolf populations recovered, and there are now more than 6000 in the continental US and over 8000 in Alaska. However, pressure from ranchers has resulted in gray wolves having their protected status removed in almost all states. According to the Wolf Conservation Center, some 1700 wolves have since been killed.

majestic herbivores graze along forest edges and are commonly sighted. More than 3000 elk roam across Rocky Mountain National Park, with a resident winter herd of 600 to 800.

Rocky Mountain National Park in northern Colorado is a special place: 'Bighorn Crossing Zone' is a sign you're unlikely to encounter anywhere else. Bighorn sheep are synonymous with the Rocky Mountains, and have made a slow but steady comeback after nearing extinction in the 1800s. Today they are sighted throughout the Rockies. During late-fall and early-winter breeding seasons, males charge each other at 20mph and clash their horns so powerfully that the sound can be heard for miles.

The open plains of eastern Oregon, Washington, Montana, Wyoming (including Yellowstone National Park) and northern Colorado are the playgrounds of the pronghorn antelope. Not technically an antelope, the pronghorn is a curious-looking, deer-like animal with two

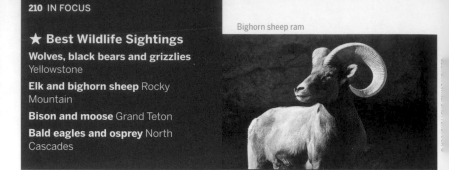

Bighorn sheep ram

★ Best Wildlife Sightings

Wolves, black bears and grizzlies
Yellowstone

Elk and bighorn sheep Rocky
Mountain

Bison and moose Grand Teton

Bald eagles and osprey North
Cascades

single black horns instead of antlers. Pronghorns belong to a unique family and are only found in the American West, but they are more famous for being able to run up to 60mph for long stretches – they're the second-fastest land animal in the world, after the cheetah.

Bears

If you see a bear on your trip to a national park, odds are it will be a black bear. These mostly vegetarian foragers are much more common than their larger, more elusive cousins, grizzly bears. Adult males weigh from 275lb to 450lb; females weigh about 175lb to 250lb. They measure 3ft high on all fours and can be taller than 5ft when standing on their hind legs. Black bears, which are sometimes brown or cinnamon colored, roam montane and subalpine forests throughout the country and are surprisingly common. The Rockies and the Sierras have the highest populations. Black bears are usually not aggressive unless there are cubs nearby, but they will go after food or food odors. Make sure to store your food and trash properly, and take a bear canister if you plan on backpacking.

The grizzly bear once ranged across the western US, but today its population in the lower 48 is estimated to be around 1500 to 1800. In the continental US, grizzlies are only found in the mountainous regions of Montana, Idaho, Wyoming and Washington. Grizzlies are classified as an endangered species in Colorado, but they are almost certainly gone from the state; the last documented grizzly in Colorado was killed in 1979. Of the national parks in the lower 48, Yellowstone has the most grizzlies, with a population of around 750 bears; you can sometimes spot them at dawn in the Lamar Valley (take a telescope or binoculars). Following flash floods in June 2022, the valley was temporarily closed to visitors, so check with the NPS for access information before you set off. Grizzlies can reach up to 800lb and can be distinguished from black bears by their concave snout, rounded ears and prominent shoulder hump.

Grizzly attacks are rare, but they do happen. Most occur because people surprise them or inadvertently come between a mother and her cub. The National Park Service (www. nps.gov) has excellent information on bears and how to handle encounters.

The best places to see bears are Yellowstone National Park and Glacier National Park.

Wolves & Coyotes

The gray wolf was once the Rocky Mountains' main predator, but relentless persecution reduced its territory to a narrow belt stretching from Canada to the Northern Rockies. The last wolf pack in Yellowstone was killed in 1924, but wolves were successfully reintroduced to the park beginning in 1995. The last official count in 2013 showed 95 wolves, though there are an estimated 400 in the Greater Yellowstone ecosystem. The Lamar Valley is your best chance for a wolf sighting, and you can sign up for a wolf-watching excursion with the Yellowstone Forever Institute (www.yellowstone.org).

Coyotes and foxes are common in many of the parks. When it comes to coyotes, you're far more likely to hear them than see them. Listening to them howl at night as you doze off to sleep is an eerie yet wonderful experience.

Cats

North America's largest cat is the mountain lion (also known as a puma or cougar), an elusive and powerful predator. There are believed to be around 40,000 mountain lions across the US, but they can be extremely difficult to see. It is the largest of any large predator in the Western Hemisphere, stretching from the Yukon in northern Canada to the southern Andes in South America. Highly adaptable, mountain lions are present in many parks, including Yellowstone, Grand Teton and Glacier. It's highly unlikely you'll spot one, as they avoid human contact. If you're camping, however, you may hear one scream – it's an utterly terrifying sound in the darkness and a virtual guarantee that you won't fall back asleep until dawn. Adult males can measure over 7ft nose to tail and weigh up to 220lb, though they are usually smaller. Though they rarely trouble humans, there are sporadic attacks every couple of years, usually involving children or joggers.

Bobcats are also present in most of these parks and are equally hard to spot.

Small Mammals

Small mammals often get short shrift on people's watch lists, but animals like beavers, pikas, marmots and river otters are a delight to see. Beavers (and their dams) are found in Rocky Mountain, Yellowstone, Grand Teton and Glacier National Parks, and are particularly fun to watch. Marmots, despite being little more than glorified ground squirrels, are enjoyable to watch hopping around on rocks in the high country. They are found in the subalpine regions of the Rockies. Other critters you might come across include bats, squirrels, voles, mice, chipmunks, raccoons, badgers, skunks, shrews and martens.

Orcas & Marine Mammals

The 'killer whale', or orca, is one of the few animals capable of attacking adult seals. This fierce predator is the largest dolphin in the world and the undisputed spirit animal of Pacific Northwest waters. Spending their entire lives in pods led by dominant females, orcas have complex societies and large brains that rival those of humans. Several resident pods live around the San Juan Islands and prey on fish, while transient pods migrate along the outer coast and hunt seals, sea lions and sometimes whales. While on a ferry around Washington's Puget Sound, keep your eyes peeled – if you're lucky you may spot a dorsal fin or two.

Anywhere on the Pacific Coast, it's hard to miss seals and sea lions. Most numerous are small, leopard-spotted harbor seals that drape themselves awkwardly over rocky headlands. From April to July, harbor seal pups may be found resting on beaches while their mothers are hunting at sea. Well-intentioned people often take these pups to animal shelters without realizing that their mothers are nearby, so it's best to leave them alone.

The much larger and darker sea lions, with external ears and the ability to 'walk' on land by shuffling on their flippers, are renowned for the thick manes and roaring cries that give them their name. Sea lions easily adapt to human presence and can be common around docks and jetties, where they sometimes steal fish from fisherfolk.

Other famous marine mammals include gray and humpback whales, which make the longest migrations of any mammals in the world. The best time to view them offshore is November to December and April to May; Depoe Bay in Oregon is an especially good place to spot them. Once hunted to near extinction, these majestic creatures have made

The Banana Slug: Don't Step on Me

While walking down a forest path in one of the Pacific Northwest's many woodsy parks, you might come across a large, yellow slug sliming slowly along the trail. Don't panic and smash it underfoot; this isn't your typical garden pest but rather the Pacific banana slug – a native slug found in damp, coastal coniferous forests from California to Alaska. Banana slugs are part of healthy ecosystems, and their food sources include decaying plants, seeds, mushrooms and dead animals.

The mascot of at least one university (UC Santa Cruz), the banana slug comes in several colors, from yellow to green to brown; many have black markings. These gastropods can be up to 10in long and are hermaphroditic (both male and female). Perhaps the most bizarre part of their mating ritual is that they often have to gnaw off each other's penises after doing the deed, so that they can then crawl away – as newly formed females.

a comeback and are a major reason for visiting the Pacific Northwest coast.

Birds

Many national parks are known for their birdwatching possibilities, but few can match Yellowstone with an estimated 316 recorded species.

Birds of prey – including eagles, falcons, hawks, owls and harriers – are common in the parks, especially the western ones. Osprey, which nest and hunt around rivers and lakes, are a commonly spotted raptor.

Keep your eyes peeled for bald eagles, which can be seen throughout the Rockies, as well as in Mt Rainier, Olympic and the North Cascades.

Most of the NPS park websites have complete bird lists – bring binoculars for the best experience.

Amphibians & Reptiles

Frogs, toads and salamanders thrive in and around streams, rivers and lakes in several of the parks. The creepy-looking Pacific giant salamander, which can reach up to 12in in length, is found in Olympic and Mt Rainier. The incredible tiger salamander has adapted to life in the barren Great Sand Dunes.

Love 'em or hate 'em, snakes are here to stay in most of the parks – but snakebites are rare (in Yellowstone, the NPS reports two in the history of the park). Western and prairie rattlesnakes are common, but they are generally docile and would rather rattle and scram than bite. Gopher and garter snakes are the most common of all.

Trees & Plants

America's national parks protect some of the greatest forests in the world. In the Pacific Northwest, in the Cascades, Mt Rainier National Park protects forests of western hemlock, Douglas fir, cedar, true firs, and western white pine. West of the Cascades, Olympic National Park is home to some of the greatest stands of temperate rain forest and old-growth forest.

In the Rockies, sparse piñon-juniper forests cover the drier, lower elevations, while the sweet-scented ponderosa pines dominate the montane zone. One of the Rockies' most striking trees is the quaking aspen, whose leaves flutter in the breeze and turn entire hillsides golden yellow in fall. The stunted, gnarled bristlecone pine, the oldest living life form on the planet, grows throughout the West just below the treeline. Many are thousands of years old.

When it comes to the smaller plants of the national parks, none seem to make an impression like wildflowers do. If you're traveling in spring or summer, it's always worth doing a little research on your park of choice to find out what's blooming when. Throughout the Rockies, June and July are prime wildflower months. In the Sierras, wildflowers bloom in spring at lower elevations.

Glacier National Park (p140)

Conservation

Protecting the national parks has been a challenge since the day Yellowstone was created in 1872. Thanks to the efforts of passionate individuals, the parks now safeguard some of the greatest natural treasures on the planet. But they face new, often concurrent, threats. Climate change, water shortages, and overuse and irresponsible land use on park peripheries all jeopardize the national parks today.

Climate Change

Major voices within the National Park Service, in agreement with scores of eminent scientists and climatologists, worry that climate change poses a significant threat to the health of the network's diverse ecosystems. Although park biologists are only just beginning to understand its impact, nearly all agree that it's taking a toll.

For example, Glacier National Park may be devoid of glaciers by 2030 if melting continues at current rates (in 1850 the park contained 150 glaciers; today there are 25).

Wildfires blamed on climate change and rising temperatures threaten many parks. A report published by the National Academy of Sciences in 2016 stated that human-caused climate change is behind the increase in wildfires in the western US, and more recent reports have only confirmed this. According to the *New York Times*, for example, summers in northern Cal-

Don't Dam the Salmon

Salmon depend on cold, clear waters during the early stages of their development. Unfortunately, logging (which creates erosion above rivers and streams) and global warming are two strikes against them. A third is dams – and the Pacific Northwest has lots of them.

Dams hurt young salmon because they slow down water, which increases its temperature and the travel time for fish to get to the ocean. Many fish are also killed by hydroelectric turbines. And on the way back – going upstream – adult salmon have a hard time getting through dams, even with fish ladders to help them.

But things are changing. Dams have been taken down on many rivers, and more are slated for removal. Even though some of these barriers aren't huge, every dam removed helps when you're a fish fighting your way upstream.

ifornia are now 2.5°F hotter than they were in the early 1970s, and nine out of the 10 biggest fires in California's history have occurred in the past 18 years. The 2016 report found the threat to be greatest in the Northwest, including Idaho, Wyoming, Montana, eastern Oregon and eastern Washington.

Park Peripheries

Aside from the impact visitors make on the parks, humans are putting immense pressure on many locations by operating high-impact businesses outside park boundaries. On Washington's Olympic Peninsula, logging companies have clear-cut forests right up to the borders of the park, which has displaced the northern spotted owl from the region. The danger is that national parks become islands of wilderness surrounded by a sea of humanity and overdevelopment.

Water

Many of the region's environmental issues revolve around water. In 2019, Lake Mead's water levels stood at just 40% of capacity. By 2022, it had dropped below 27%.

Water also has the potential to create regional tension, as desert states downstream of the Rockies compete for this increasingly limited resource. In 2019, in the midst of what the New York Times described as a 19-year drought, seven western US states (Arizona, California, Colorado, Nevada, New Mexico, Utah and Wyoming) signed an agreement to voluntarily cut their water use to sustainably manage supply from the Colorado River, prevent Lake Mead from running dry, and avoid federal government intervention. An estimated 40 million people rely on the Colorado River for their water.

Visiting National Parks

As magnificent as the nation's national parks are, only a tiny percentage of the US national budget is put aside for their benefit. Despite this, park visitors can make a positive impact by traveling sustainably and getting involved with park associations. Whenever you can, ride park shuttles instead of driving your car. Skip high-impact park activities such as snowmobiling in Yellowstone. Conserve water and prevent erosion by always staying on trails. If you're backpacking, use biodegradable soaps (or skip them altogether) and follow the principles of Leave No Trace (www.lnt.org).

Nearly every national park has an associated foundation or other nonprofit that supports its parent park. These organizations, which include Yellowstone Forever (www.yellowstone.org), conduct everything from trail maintenance to habitat restoration. Members can volunteer or donate to programs that are critical to the parks' wellbeing.

The National Parks Conservation Association (www.npca.org) covers all of the parks. Since 1919, this nonprofit organization has been protecting and preserving America's national parks through research, advocacy and education.

★ Did you know?

More than 200 national parks and monuments contain at least one endangered species.

Top: Yellowstone National Park (p178); Bottom left: Bison, Grand Teton National Park (p152); Bottom right: Geyser, Yellowstone National Park (p178)

Canary Springs, Yellowstone National Park (p181)

Landscapes & Geology

Tectonic collisions, glaciation, volcanic eruptions, erosion – the forces of nature and time have worked wonders on the continent, and nowhere is that geological history more beautifully evident than in the national parks. Each park tells its own ancient story through landscapes that are as unique as they are complex.

Rocky Mountains

Running from British Columbia (Canada) to northern New Mexico, the Rocky Mountains are North America's longest chain of mountains. They begin their dramatic ascent from the western reaches of the Great Plains and climb to over 14,000ft.

More than 100 separate ranges make up the Rockies. Most were uplifted during the Laramide orogeny, which began around 80 million years ago when a chunk of oceanic crust took a shallow dive under the continental plate, bumping along just under the surface of the Earth. This movement forced the Rockies upwards, sideways and in some cases on top of themselves – such as at the Lewis Overthrust Fault in Glacier National Park, where older rock, miles thick, was pushed some 50 miles across the top of younger rock. Over time, glaciers and erosion have worn the peaks down to their present form, revealing rock layers that betray their long and chaotic past. The process of forming the Rockies continued until the Pleistocene ice age of two million years ago, when they were hewn by glaciers into the landscapes we see today.

With the retreat of the glaciers at the end of the last ice age, the Rockies became more hospitable to life, though they still see extremes of weather. During winter months much of the Rockies is covered under several feet of snow. Although this is a burden on large mammals who have to migrate to lower areas to find food – or instead choose to hibernate through the winter, as bears do – it's a boon for skiers and snowboarders, who revel in the light, fluffy continental snow pack. Words such as 'champagne powder' and 'cold smoke' are the envy of Pacific Coast skiers.

Yellowstone was shaped by the same ice age, but what really differentiates it from other parks in the range is its volcanic activity. Yellowstone sits on a geological 'hot spot,' a thin piece of the earth's crust that is essentially floating atop a massive, 125-mile-deep plume of molten rock. Fueled by this underground furnace, Yellowstone bubbles like a pot on a hot stove to produce over 10,000 geothermal features – more than all other geothermal areas on the planet combined.

Wilderness Areas in the Rockies

All wilderness areas protect unique lands worth visiting. Among our favorites:

Frank Church–River of No Return, Idaho The largest contiguous wilderness in the lower 48 protects the world-famous Middle Fork of the Salmon River watershed.

Bob Marshall Wilderness Complex, Montana Home to the densest population of grizzly bears outside of Alaska.

Absaroka-Beartooth, Montana and Wyoming Includes the rugged mountains to the northeast of Yellowstone, extending habitat protection of the Greater Yellowstone ecosystem.

Weminuche Wilderness Area, Colorado The largest wilderness in Colorado is home to three of the state's 14ers and is most easily accessed by historic train.

Bridger Wilderness, Wyoming Hundreds of glassy alpine lakes and the granite spires of the Wind River Range draw climbers from around the world.

Yellowstone, Grand Teton, Glacier, Rocky Mountain, Black Canyon and the Great Sand Dunes together protect some 3 million acres of the Rockies. Rocky Mountain has the highest point in these parks, its iconic Longs Peak punching 14,259ft into the sky.

Wilderness with a Capital 'W'

Imagine a place where you can hike for miles and never cross a road; you can camp for days and never hear a chainsaw; you can paddle for a week and never see a motorboat or pass a town. Now, imagine that this fantastic place is guaranteed to stay that way forever. Nature – purely wild – completely protected. Welcome to Wilderness with a capital 'W,' an incredible concept that already exists.

In 1964 a group of far-thinking individuals convinced Congress to pass the Wilderness Act, a brilliant piece of legislation that protects special areas of our public lands from development. The law states, in part: 'A wilderness, in contrast with those areas where man and his own works dominate the landscape, is hereby recognized as an area where the earth and its community of life are untrammeled by man, where man himself is a visitor who does not remain.'

Congress set an example for the world by recognizing that some wild landscapes are more important than economic development and expansion. They are vital to the health of the country and its people.

You can explore wilderness areas throughout the Rocky Mountain West; consult with the local Forest Service office to plan your journey. Just remember: no motorized vehicles or bicycles are allowed inside. Lace up your boots instead, or saddle up a horse.

Pacific Northwest

North of the Sierra Nevada stands the Cascade Range, a volcanic mountain range stretching from northern California into British Columbia. The range's highest peak is 14,411ft Mt Rainier, a massive stratovolcano protected by Mt Rainier National Park. The volcano is 'episodically active' and is considered the most hazardous volcano in the Cascades. The mountain is covered in snow for much of the year and contains expansive ice fields and 25 glaciers. It last erupted in 1854. Other major parks in the range include Oregon's Crater Lake – an extinct volcano whose caldera filled with water 7700 years ago and is today the deepest (and clearest) lake in the US – and the North Cascades, a rugged swathe of glacier-bound jagged peaks, featuring both temperate rainforest on the west side of the range and drier ponderosa forests on the east.

West of the Cascades, on Washington's Olympic Peninsula, the Olympic Mountains plunge dramatically into the Pacific Ocean. They are a separate range entirely and, unlike the volcanic Cascades, were formed five to 15 million years ago during convergence of the Juan de Fuca and North American plates. Between the Olympic's highest peaks, which top out at 7965ft, and the ocean below, Olympic National Park protects a landscape drenched in rain, hammered by wind and pounded by waves.

Fire & Ice: A Geologic History of the Pacific Northwest

From 16 to 13 million years ago, eastern Oregon and Washington witnessed one of the premier episodes of volcanic activity in earth's history. Due to shifting stresses in the earth's crust, much of interior western North America began cracking along thousands of lines and releasing enormous amounts of lava that flooded over the landscape. On multiple occasions, so much lava was produced that it filled the Columbia River channel and reached the Oregon coast, forming prominent headlands like Cape Lookout. Today, hardened lava flows can be seen at places such as Newberry National Volcanic Monument and the McKenzie Pass Area, in central Oregon; for

The Continental Divide

Along numerous roads across the Rockies, you'll see a sign announcing that you're crossing the Continental Divide. Despite lying so far west, so high are the Rockies that this marks the geological dividing line of the continental USA. What that means is simple: rivers west of that point drain into the Pacific, while those to the east head for the Atlantic. While this mostly holds, there are one or two exceptions to this rule. One is Triple Divide Peak (8020 ft) in Montana's Glacier National Park: rain that falls and ice that melts on this mountain reach both the Pacific and the Atlantic, with some also making its way north into Hudson Bay for good measure.

To take a closer look at it all, consider the 3100-mile Continental Divide Trail (www.continentaldividetrail.org), an epic hike that passes through Montana, Idaho, Wyoming, Colorado and New Mexico, including through Rocky Mountain, Yellowstone and Glacier National Parks.

a cool lava tube, head to Mt St Helens Ape Cave, in Washington.

The ice ages of the past two million years created a massive ice field from Washington to BC – and virtually every mountain range in the rest of the region was blanketed by glaciers. Even more dramatically, tongues of ice extending southward out of Canada prevented the 3000-sq-mile glacial Lake Missoula in present-day Montana from draining. Consequently, on about 40 separate occasions, these massive ice dams burst, releasing more water than all the world's rivers combined and flooding much of eastern Washington up to 1000ft deep. Grand Coulee and Dry Falls of northeastern Washington are remnants of these spectacular floods, as are the crowd-pleasing waterfalls (such as Multnomah Falls) of the Columbia River Gorge that plummet over cliffs carved by the floods.

Fun Facts

The largest national park is Alaska's Wrangell-St Elias. Bigger than Switzerland, it's also home to the second-tallest peak in the US, Mt St Elias (18,008 ft), whose dizzying climb from sea level occurs in just 10 miles.

Colorado's Great Sand Dunes are composed of 29 different rocks and minerals – from obsidian and sulfur to amethyst and turquoise – and cover an incredible 30 sq miles of land, with dunes as tall as 700ft.

Alaska

Dramatic mountain ranges arch across the landmass of Alaska. The Pacific Mountain System, which includes the Alaska, Aleutian and St Elias Ranges, as well as the Chugach and Kenai Mountains, sweeps along the south before dipping into the sea southwest of Kodiak Island. Most of Alaska's seven national parks are located here, including the granddaddy of them all, Denali – its namesake mountain is North America's tallest peak (20,310ft). Further north looms the imposing and little-visited Brooks Range, skirting the Arctic Circle, where you'll find the wild and remote Gates of the Arctic.

In between the Alaska and Brooks Ranges is interior Alaska, an immense plateau rippled by foothills, low mountains and magnificent rivers; among them the third longest in the US, the mighty Yukon River, which runs for 2300 miles. At the state's far southeastern corner is Glacier Bay – the perfect place to observe glacial retreat in action.

In geological terms Alaska is relatively young and still very active. The state represents the northern boundary of the chain of Pacific Ocean volcanoes known as the Ring of Fire and is the most seismically active region of North America. In fact, Alaska claims 52% of the earthquakes that occur in the country and averages more than 13 each day. Most are mild shakes, but some are deadly. Three of the six largest earthquakes in the world – and seven of the 10 largest in the US – have occurred in Alaska.

Top: Longs Peak, Rocky Mountain National Park (p172);
Bottom left: Bison, Yellowstone National Park (p178);
Bottom right: Iceberg Lake, Glacier National Park (p144)

Behind the Scenes

Acknowledgements

Climate map data adapted from Peel MC, Finlayson BL & McMahon TA (2007) 'Updated World Map of the Köppen-Geiger Climate Classification', *Hydrology and Earth System Sciences*, 11, pp1633–44.

Cover photograph: Wildflowers, Mt Rainier, Alexey Smolyanyy/ Shutterstock ©

This Book

This 1st edition of Lonely Planet's *Rocky Mountains & Pacific Northwest's National Parks* was researched and written by Anthony Ham, Greg Benchwick, Catherin Bodry, Celeste Brash, Gregor Clark, Michael Grosberg, Adam Karlin, Bradley Mayhew, Carolyn McCarthy, Becky Ohlsen, Brendan Sainsbury, Regis St Louis, Benedict Walker and Karla Zimmerman.

This guidebook was produced by the following:

Commissioning Editor Angela Tinson

Design Development Katherine Marsh

Cartographic Series Designer Wayne Murphy

Production Editor Sofie Andersen

Cartographer Julie Sheridan

Book Designer Aomi Ito

Assisting Editors Andrea Dobbin, Soo Hamilton, Alison Killilea, Etty Payne

Production Development Liz Heynes, Dianne Schallmeiner, John Taufa, Juan Winata

Cover Researcher Gwen Cotter

Thanks to Ronan Abayawickrema, Melanie Dankel, Clare Healy, Sonia Kapoor

---

Send Us Your Feedback

We love to hear from travelers – your comments keep us on our toes and help make our books better. Our well-traveled team reads every word on what you loved or loathed about this book. Although we cannot reply individually to your submissions, we always guarantee that your feedback goes straight to the appropriate authors, in time for the next edition. Each person who sends us information is thanked in the next edition.

Visit lonelyplanet.com/contact to submit your updates and suggestions or to ask for help. Our award-winning website also features inspirational travel stories and news.

Note: We may edit, reproduce and incorporate your comments in Lonely Planet products such as guidebooks, websites and digital products, so let us know if you are happy to have your name acknowledged. For a copy of our privacy policy visit lonelyplanet.com/legal

Index

Carolyn McCarthy

Carolyn specializes in travel, culture and adventure in the Americas. She has written for *National Geographic, Outside, BBC Magazine, Sierra Magazine, Boston Globe* and other publications. A former Fulbright fellow and Banff Mountain Grant recipient, she has documented life in the most remote corners of Latin America. Carolyn has contributed to 40 guidebooks and anthologies for Lonely Planet, including *Colorado, USA, Argentina, Chile, Trekking in the Patagonian Andes, Panama, Peru* and *USA National Parks* guides. For more information, visit www.carolynmccarthy.org or follow her Instagram travels @mccarthyoffmap.

Brendan Sainsbury

Born and raised in the UK in a town that never merits a mention in any guidebook (Andover, Hampshire), Brendan spent the holidays of his youth caravanning in the English Lake District and didn't leave Blighty until he was 19. Making up for lost time, he's since squeezed 70 countries into a sometimes precarious existence as a writer and professional vagabond. In the last 11 years, he has written more than 40 books for Lonely Planet about places ranging from from Castro's Cuba to the canyons of Peru.

Regis St Louis

Regis grew up in a small town in the American Midwest – the kind of place that fuels big dreams of travel – and he developed an early fascination with foreign dialects and world cultures. He spent his formative years learning Russian and a handful of Romance languages, which served him well on journeys across much of the globe. Regis has contributed to more than 50 Lonely Planet titles, covering destinations across six continents. His travels have taken him from the mountains of Kamchatka to remote island villages in Melanesia, and to many grand urban landscapes. When not on the road, he lives in New Orleans. Follow him @regisstlouis on Instagram.

Contributing Writers

Catherin Bodry, Celeste Brash, Gregor Clark, Adam Karlin, Becky Ohlsen, Benedict Walker, Karla Zimmerman

Symbols & Map Key

These symbols and abbreviations give vital information for each listing:

🌱 Sustainable or green recommendation
FREE No payment required

📞 Telephone number	🏊 Swimming pool
🕐 Opening hours	🚌 Bus
🅿 Parking	⛴ Ferry
❄ Air-conditioning	🚊 Tram
📶 Wi-fi access	🚆 Train
	👪 Family-friendly

Find your best experiences with these Great For... icons.

🏖 Beaches		📷 Photo Op	
🚲 Cycling		🔭 Scenery	
👨‍👩‍👧 Family Travel		🚶 Walking	
📖 History		❄ Winter Travel	
🦫 Wildlife			

Points of Interest

- 🏖 Beach
- 🏕 Camping
- 🛶 Canoeing/Kayaking
- 🍷 Drinking & Nightlife
- 🍴 Eating
- 🏠 Hut/Shelter
- 🔭 Lookout
- ▲ Mountain/Volcano
- ❗ Monument
- 🏛 Museum/Gallery/ Historic Building
- 🌳 Park

- ⊗ Ruin
- 🛍 Shopping
- ⛷ Skiing
- 🛏 Sleeping
- 🚶 Walking
- 🐾 Zoo/Wildlife Sanctuary
- ◉ Other Sight
- ✛ Other Activity
- ● Other Point of Interest
-)(Pass
- 🧺 Picnic Area
- 💧 Springs/Waterfall

Information & Transport

- ✈ Airport
- ⊗ Border crossing
- 🚌 Bus
- ⊕ Cable car/Funicular
- 🚲 Cycling
- ⊖ Ferry
- Ⓜ Metro station

- 🅿 Parking
- ⛽ Petrol station
- 🚻 Toilet
- ℹ Tourist Information
- 🚉 Train station/Railway
- ● Other Information/ Transport

Our Story

A beat-up old car, a few dollars in the pocket and a sense of adventure. In 1972 that's all Tony and Maureen Wheeler needed for the trip of a lifetime – across Europe and Asia overland to Australia. It took several months, and at the end – broke but inspired – they sat at their kitchen table writing and stapling together their first travel guide, *Across Asia on the Cheap*. Within a week they'd sold 1500 copies. Lonely Planet was born.

Today, Lonely Planet has offices in the US, Ireland and China, with a network of over 2000 contributors in every corner of the globe. We share Tony's belief that 'a great guidebook should do three things: inform, educate and amuse'.

Our Writers

Anthony Ham

Anthony is a freelance writer who travels the world in search of stories. His particular passions are the wildlife, wild places and wide-open spaces of the planet, from the Great Plains of the US to the Amazon, East and Southern Africa, and the Arctic. He writes for magazines and newspapers around the world, and his book *The Last Lions of Africa* was published in 2020.

Greg Benchwick

Greg has been drifting across the high plains of the Colorado Plateau for most of his life – he calls it a 'true spiritual home'. As a kid, he canoed desolate river canyons with his family, while in his wild college days he pushed the limits on classic rock-climbing routes like Castleton Tower and the Moonlight Buttress. He's back-packed lost canyons, hitchhiked to Zion, mountain-biked Moab, and found solitude and peace in the lost corners of this desert wonderworld.

Michael Grosberg

Michael has worked on over 50 Lonely Planet guidebooks. Other international work included development on Rota in the western Pacific; South Africa where he investigated and wrote about political violence and trained newly elected government representatives; and Quito, Ecuador, to teach. He received a Masters in Comparative Literature and taught literature and writing as an adjunct professor.

Bradley Mayhew

Bradley has been writing guidebooks for 20 years now. He started traveling while studying Chinese at Oxford University, and he is the co-author of Lonely Planet's *Tibet, Nepal, Trekking in the Nepal Himalaya, Bhutan, Central Asia* and many others. Bradley has also fronted two TV series for Arte and SWR, one retracing the route of Marco Polo via Turkey, Iran, Afghanistan, Central Asia and China, and the other trekking Europe's 10 most scenic long-distance trails.

◄─────────── More Writers ◄───────────

STAY IN TOUCH LONELYPLANET.COM/CONTACT

IRELAND
Digital Depot, Digital Hub
Roe Lane (off Thomas St)
Dublin 8, D08 TCV4

 twitter.com/
lonelyplanet

 facebook.com/
lonelyplanet

instagram.com/
lonelyplanet

youtube.com/
lonelyplanet

lonelyplanet.com/
newsletter